THE SUCCESSFUL COLLEGE ATHLETIC PROGRAM
The New Standard

John R. Gerdy

AMERICAN COUNCIL ON EDUCATION ★
ORYX PRESS ★
Series on Higher Education
1997

37201320

The rare Arabian oryx is believed to have inspired the myth of the unicorn. This desert antelope became virtually extinct in the early 1960s. At that time several groups of international conservationists arranged to have 9 animals sent to the Phoenix Zoo to be the nucleus of a captive breeding herd. Today the oryx population is over 1,000, and over 500 have been returned to the Middle East.

© 1997 by American Council on Education and The Oryx Press
Published by The Oryx Press
4041 North Central at Indian School Road
Phoenix, Arizona 85012-3397

Published simultaneously in Canada
Printed and bound in the United States of America

∞ The paper used in this publication meets the minimum requirements of the American National Standard for Information Sciences—Permanence of Paper for Printed Library Materials, ANSI Z39.48-1984.

Library of Congress Cataloging-in-Publication Data
Gerdy, John R.
    The successful college athletic program: the new standard / John R. Gerdy.
    p. cm.—(American Council on Education/Oryx Press series on higher education)
    Includes bibliographical references and index.
    ISBN 1-57356-109-6 (alk. paper)
    1. College sports—Standards—United States. 2. Education, Higher—Aims and objectives—United States. I. Title. II. Series.
GV351.G47   1997
796.04'3'0973—1997   97-22605
                                                                 CIP

CONTENTS

ACKNOWLEDGMENTS

I am grateful to all those who took the time to discuss ideas or review drafts of chapters, especially Jim Bruning, Kevin Lennon, Britton Banowsky, Bob Bradley, Tom Burish, Walt Newsom, Greg Sankey, Bob McKillop, Willie Marble, Cynthia Patterson, Hoke Wilder, Fred Dressel, Bob McCabe, Maureen Devlin, and Lane Estes. Their time, encouragement, and thoughtful comments are always greatly appreciated. I am also very thankful for the patience and support of Duana Koonce, who spent much time transcribing my often incoherent tapes and barely legible notes, and to Todd Petr and Craig Jaffe for their assistance in obtaining research data. The editorial assistance of John Wagner and Leslie Crenna was invaluable. Portions of this book are adapted from articles I have published in journals. The articles are listed in the bibliography. On those articles, I was the fortunate recipient of valuable comments from colleagues, friends, and editors too numerous to mention.

I also wish to thank Jim Murray and Susan Slesinger for not only believing in the project but challenging me to make it better.

To Wallace, whose many "interruptions" were always joyous, and my wife Follin, whose sharp editorial eye has made me a better writer and whose love and support have made me a better person, I give a heart-felt thank you.

INTRODUCTION

The significant problems we face cannot be solved at the same level of thinking we were at when we created them.

Albert Einstein

It might seem ironic that a quote from Albert Einstein would be used to set the tone for a book about intercollegiate athletics. All biographies indicate that Einstein did not have much of a jump shot, could not bench press half his weight, and certainly could not "turn the corner" quickly enough to rush for more than 100 yards on a Saturday afternoon in the fall. This book, however, is not about athletics: it is about education. Although some will claim that college athletics *is* about education, most people, including many of those involved in college athletics, do not think of education when they hear the term "college athletics." That must change.

Although the media, society, and higher education, as well as many of those involved in intercollegiate athletics, have trivialized athletics as simply entertainment, college athletics has the potential to become a significant contributor to the higher education team. Because of its visibility and tremendous influence in our society, college athletics' potential to promote educational excellence and provide educational leadership is enormous. So, at a time when athletics seems most divorced from the educational process—appears most trivialized as simply entertainment—it can be more central to the future health and prosperity of higher education than it has ever been. To date, however, it is questionable whether we have been responsible in the way we have used its potentially far-reaching influence.

While associate commissioner for Compliance and Academic Affairs at the Southeastern Conference, my responsibility was to encourage athletic department personnel to consider and respect, at all times and in everything they did, institutional and academic integrity and student-athlete welfare. This role often placed me in the position of challenging coaches and administrators to justify many of the beliefs they held dear. I cannot recall the number of times, when challenging "the way things had always been done," I was asked why I wanted to "tear down" and "destroy" athletics. Nothing could have been further from my mind. I had no desire to destroy athletics. I am, after all, a product of the system. My experience as a Division I student-athlete ranks as one of the most enjoyable and educational experiences of my life. But simply because my experience was positive does not mean that there are not problems with the system. For others, the experience was not so positive. And, with the influence of television and advertisers, the pressure to win and to generate revenue—forces that increasingly influence the long-term educational and personal interests of the student-athlete in a negative way—has only intensified.

Numerous books have cavalierly criticized college athletics without offering thoughtful and realistic suggestions for improvement. While this book references many of the "ills" of college athletics, I have not set out to point fingers at individuals. As a member of the college athletic community, I have been a part of the system for which these changes are proposed, and I consider myself a part of the system still with changes of my own to make. Shortfalls are cited simply to illustrate the need for the proposed changes that I have suggested in this book—changes designed to strengthen college athletics, to make it better. I want college athletics to remain vibrant, relevant, and strong so that my daughter and thousands of other young people will continue to have the opportunity to achieve a positive, well-balanced intercollegiate athletic experience. So rather than viewing this work as an indictment of college athletics, I would prefer to consider it a challenge to the higher education community—those of us who care deeply about athletics' place in that community—to consider what college athletics should, could, and must be about.

I have attempted to define the ideal. In doing so, there is the risk that some will immediately dismiss what I have presented as simply pie-eyed, idealistic pipe dreams that have no place in the real world of college athletics. But I have lived in the real world of college athletics. While based upon some fundamental and other idealistic principles, the suggestions offered are realistic and achievable. Pipe dreams are important; unless and until we define the ideal, there is no chance to progress toward a better way of doing things.

The college athletics referred to in the following pages is intercollegiate, as opposed to intramural or club athletics, and primarily NCAA Division I rather than NCAA Divisions II, III, or NAIA. While the points made apply to athletics at any level, having been a former NCAA Division I student-athlete and administrator, this is the "college athletics" with which I am most familiar. Further, it is at the NCAA Division I level, particularly in the sports of football and basketball, that most of the well-documented ills of intercollegiate athletics occur. More important, athletics at this level has the greatest potential to contribute to higher education's mission in new, exciting, and far-reaching ways.

Why confuse fun and games—which is what far too many people think of college athletics—with educational leadership? This question must be at the core of any discussion regarding the future of intercollegiate athletics because if athletics is viewed as having no connection to the overall university, no redeeming value within the higher education setting, it is no longer useful and should not exist in that setting. In many ways, athletics is like the seven-foot, 280-pound basketball player with unlimited athletic potential who is an enormous source of frustration for his coach because he prefers to spend time practicing saxophone rather than jump shots—or dreams of being a medical doctor rather than the next "Dr. J." Lots of potential to contribute to the team, but what the coach would describe as an "under-achiever."

The challenges facing higher education are too daunting for such under-achievement. Our colleges and universities have, among other things, been called upon to retrain our country's workforce to compete in today's global economy, address issues related to its growing diversity, and restore a sense of ethical awareness and civic responsibility in its young people. Further, higher education is facing these challenges in an environment of declining public trust and decreasing resources.

To meet these challenges, higher education must use every one of its resources to its fullest potential, including athletics. Thus, the time has come to look beyond the traditional role of athletics and reassess how it can contribute more directly to higher education's mission. To do so, however, will require "a new level of thinking," as suggested by Einstein. We must raise our level of thinking regarding athletics' role in higher education from athletics as simply entertainment and business to athletics as a tool to teach and a vehicle to promote broad educational and institutional goals.

In short, we must begin to think at a new level.

Reference

Covey, Stephen R. 1989. Quote from Einstein in *The Seven Habits of Highly Effective People.* New York: Simon and Schuster, p. 42.

PART ONE

• • • • • • • • • • •

Our Past

CHAPTER 1

The New Standard

The national publicity associated with scandals at a handful of universities with big-time varsity sports programs has a disproportionate influence on public images and opinions of all colleges and universities. The media attention afforded big games and big scandals dominates and distorts the popular image of what American higher education is all about. The most serious concern is that flagrant, sustained abuses in college sports programs lead to the erosion of public faith in institutions of higher education.

John R. Thelin and Lawrence L. Wiseman
*The Old College Try: Balancing Academics and Athletics in
Higher Education*

Roy Kramer, commissioner of the Southeastern Conference, often tells of a visit he had with Colonel Tom Elam following a basketball game between Vanderbilt University and the University of Tennessee. Kramer was athletic director at Vanderbilt at the time, and Elam, an old country lawyer from East Tennessee, was chairman of the Athletic Board at Tennessee. Vanderbilt had won the game to sweep the season series from the Volunteers. While offering Kramer congratulations, Elam was approached by a large man dressed from head to foot in Tennessee orange—orange overalls and hat, and even orange shoes. The fan grabbed Elam, swung him around, and barked, "What the hell we gonna do about this, Colonel Tom?" Elam paused, looked him straight in the eye, and replied, "Well, we could close the university" (Kramer 1996).

Although difficult for many fans to understand, the university does not exist for the sole purpose of sponsoring a football or basketball team. While its entertainment value and the sense of pride a college athletic team can instill in a state or region ought not be underemphasized, many within and outside academe question the place of athletics in higher education. The concern is that athletic programs are about winning, making money, and providing entertainment rather than about education and, as a result, are not contributing to the mission of the university in significant ways.

One of the greatest challenges facing educational leaders today is the task of reversing a decline in public trust in higher education. While our athletic departments are not alone in contributing to this decline, they have certainly done their part. Scandals involving athletic departments across the nation are well documented and widely publicized. As of December 1996, 28 athletic programs were on NCAA probation. Most recently, the University of Louisville's men's basketball program was placed on probation for violations of NCAA rules governing extra benefits, preferential treatment, and recruiting. Texas Southern University was cited for a lack of institutional control for violations of rules governing academic eligibility, extra benefits, and ethical conduct. And UCLA's head basketball coach, Jim Harrick, was fired for violating an NCAA recruiting rule and then lying about it. But athletic scandals are not limited to those that result in NCAA sanctions. Boston College was embroiled in 1996 in a scandal in which various members of its football team were caught gambling on college football games, in some cases, on games involving their own team. At the University of Rhode Island, a group of football players attacked a fraternity house and its members in a particularly violent display of team unity.

The purpose of this book, however, is not to rehash athletic department breaches of institutional or NCAA ethics and standards of behavior. These transgressions are merely symptomatic of a larger problem—the alienation of athletics from the educational mission of the university. Suffice it to say that what transpires in athletic departments greatly affects the image of the individual institution and consequently the public trust in higher education generally.

The purpose of this book is to explore and illustrate how athletics can be more effectively used to assist higher education in fulfilling its mission and, in the process, to justify more fully its place in academe.

NOT NECESSARILY "REFORM" BUT "REFOCUS"

It is no secret what the fundamental purpose of athletics within higher education should be. One need look no further than page one of the *1996-97 NCAA Manual* to find that purpose outlined as one of the NCAA's two most fundamental policies. NCAA Constitution, Article 1, reads as follows:

1.3.1 Basic Purpose. The competitive athletics programs of member institutions are designed to be a vital part of the educational system. A basic purpose of this Association is to maintain intercollegiate athletics as an integral part of the educational program and the athlete as an integral part of the student body and, by doing so, retain a clear line of demarcation between intercollegiate athletics and professional sports.

This purpose, along with the NCAA's second fundamental policy, which states that member institutions are obligated to enforce the rules of the association, are clear. Further, they are elaborated upon in NCAA Constitution, Article 2, titled "Principles for Conduct of Intercollegiate Athletics." Some of the principles outlined in this section are institutional control, student-athlete welfare, sportsmanship and ethical conduct, sound academic standards, amateurism, and rules compliance. With guidelines clearly stated, the problem is not that those in college athletics do not understand the principles upon which athletic programs should operate.

If these principles are so obvious, why is it that public skepticism regarding athletics' place in higher education remains so high? Why are these principles seemingly so hard for athletics professionals to implement? Where have we gone wrong?

Simply put, those of us involved with athletic programs, from university administrators on down, have lost our focus. While well aware of what athletics should be, we continue to allow the principles set out in the NCAA Constitution to be compromised in the name of more television dollars, championship banners, personal financial gain, and ego gratification. We have lost sight of our overall purpose.

Certainly, the NCAA has taken some significant steps toward reform. For example, since 1984, changes have been made in the NCAA's governance structure to ensure more effective presidential control. Both initial and continuing eligibility standards have been raised periodically. Institutions are now required to report on how many of their student-athletes ultimately graduate. In addition, efforts to improve institutional control have also intensified. Athletic dorms have been eliminated, and practice time required of athletes has been limited to 20 hours per week. In 1995, Division I institutions began an NCAA certification program designed to help institutions assess how well their athletic programs met national standards in the areas of governance, academic integrity, fiscal integrity, and equity.

These reform initiatives, while representing progress, are nonetheless piecemeal in nature. Most of them address only the symptoms of athletic department abuse—such as recruiting violations, academic fraud, and excessive time demands placed upon student-athletes—rather than the root causes of athletics' alienation from the academic community. Thus, the purpose of this book is not to point out means of reforming college athletics with a laundry list of specific rule changes, but rather it is to challenge the community of higher education to bring back into focus its purpose, standards of conduct, and the way in which it will operate intercollegiate athletic programs.

While many of the initiatives outlined in the pages that follow represent new perspectives regarding the way in which athletics are perceived, conducted, and managed, other suggestions are modeled after long-agreed-upon and codified NCAA principles. Athletic programs must exist as an integral part of the higher education community. Student-athletes must routinely become an integral part of the student body and their coaches a part of the academic community. All athletic department personnel must act in accordance not only with the specific rules of the NCAA, but also with general principles regarding sportsmanship and ethical conduct. These principles are sound and are not in need of major reform. We do, however, need to pay renewed attention to them. We must look at them with a new perspective to gain a better sense of how these purposes interface with the greater purposes of the academic institution. Since it can be argued that the athletic community is not in full compliance with these greater purposes, we must refocus at a fundamental level upon the soundness and importance of these principles. In short, we must redouble our efforts to accomplish what we have long claimed as our primary justifications.

For example, we must distinguish between what coaches and athletic administrators *do*, which is conduct games, and what they are *about*, which is education. Games, statistics, and scores are relatively meaningless. Newspaper clippings fade, and trophies tarnish. By the time this year's championship game is played, most people will have forgotten who participated in last year's. What has lasting significance, however, is the way in which athletics can positively affect the lives of those who play and those who watch. If the greater purpose is not clearly understood and fully embraced by coaches and athletic administrators, college athletics will continue to be trivialized as simply entertainment, with no deeper or more compelling rationale for its existence than that it provides Saturday afternoon entertainment.

Due to the previously mentioned decline in public trust, as well as increasingly difficult financial circumstances, each and every component of the higher education community is being challenged to streamline operations and justify its worth to the university. To think that athletics is not going to be held to the same standard of utility as the English department or the school of medicine is dangerously presumptuous. Thus, the biggest future challenge facing college athletics is the need for the leaders of the athletic department and of higher education in general to demonstrate to an increasingly skeptical public that athletic programs do in fact contribute to the purpose of American higher education in relevant and timely ways.

Despite what that devoted Tennessee fan wearing all orange may think, our colleges will continue to educate, to produce quality research, and to serve the community with or without big-time athletics.

The real purpose of this book, then, is to examine the ways that athletics can contribute more directly to higher education's three-pronged purpose of teaching, research, and service. Such an effort is necessary because the conventional ways in which we have explained the value of athletics to the educational community are no longer enough to convince an increasingly skeptical public, media, and academic community that big-time athletics makes a valuable contribution to higher education.

REDEFINING GOALS

Athletic department success has traditionally been measured by championship banners and revenue generated. But at a time when higher education is struggling to address issues relating to poverty, illiteracy, and environmental degradation, in an increasingly diverse, complex, and technologically sophisticated world, championship banners are virtually meaningless. Thus, it is the responsibility of academic leaders to establish an athletic department incentive and measurement system that rewards behavior that contributes more directly to higher education's mission. In short, it is time for American higher education to embrace the New Standard for determining athletic department success.

Organizations inevitably evolve to achieve that for which they are rewarded. Inasmuch as athletic departments have been rewarded principally for the purpose of winning games, they have evolved to emphasize achievement of this goal to the detriment of all others. A more meaningful standard, however, would be to measure athletic department success in terms of contributions to its institution's efforts to meet the many challenges facing higher education and the society it is meant to serve. This New Standard of success will allow for the more effective realization of conventional justifications, as well as the development of new purposes that are more relevant for the world in which higher education exists today.

But implementing the New Standard will not be easy, nor will it happen overnight. Fundamental changes in the way athletics is perceived and managed by both the athletic and the academic communities must occur for the New Standard to take hold. It will require an honest, critical self-assessment and a willingness to consider new ideas and principles. It will also require a level of thinking that all other attempts at athletics reform have yet to demand.

Before the specific components of the New Standard can be implemented, the entire higher education community must be challenged, as

Einstein suggests, "to think at a new level" regarding the role, purpose, and potential of athletics. This shift in the way in which we approach the role of athletics on campus must occur not only within athletic departments but throughout the entire higher education community. And the first application of Einstein's challenge must apply to the consideration of the following four ideological principles.

INSTITUTIONAL TEAMWORK

Virtually every campus that sponsors big-time college sports has a division between the athletic and academic communities. On some campuses, a wary relationship exists. On others, the relationship can be classified as hostile. It is time to break down these barriers and work together to address the many issues facing higher education. Simply put, the athletic and academic communities must realize that they are on the same team and that as teammates they have a responsibility to work together for the good of the team. With such serious challenges facing our society, and hence higher education, doing anything less would be irresponsible.

Coaches and athletic administrators must realize that athletics is not bigger, better, or more important than the university. Although it might be easy to lose perspective with the media and fans saying otherwise, athletics would not exist without the university. Therefore, athletics must become a part of the team. The concept of teamwork as a primary justification for athletics should be easy for coaches and athletic administrators because their business is to teach teamwork. As hard as the criticism may be to accept, athletics has not been a good team player in higher education, and it is time for that to change.

The academic community, on the other hand, must stop looking down its nose at athletics as if it were a meaningless activity. Just as much, and in many cases more, can be learned on the playing field as is learned in the classroom; athletic lessons in discipline, team work, and perseverance can be applied to life off the field. If faculty and academic administrators do not believe that athletics, with its tremendous visibility and influence in our society, can contribute in meaningful and vibrant ways to the mission of the university, they need to take note of the tens of thousands of people who attend games on their campuses and the millions who watch them on television. Athletics can be a tremendous educational resource. To dismiss it as trivial is to waste it.

As members of the same team, the athletic and the academic communities must begin to work together to implement the New Standard.

THE MANAGEMENT OF ATHLETICS

The traditional attitude of academic leaders toward athletics has been to simply hope that the university will not be damaged by a highly visible athletic scandal. As long as athletic departments kept their business confined to the sports pages and off of the front page, college and university presidents have not been inclined to meddle in athletic department affairs. As a result, athletic departments have expended considerable effort and resources to comply with NCAA rules to stay scandal free. While these preventive measures are important, such an overwhelmingly defensive approach to managing athletics has resulted in a lack of attention and resources being applied to identifying and developing proactive, aggressive ways in which athletics can contribute to the university's educational purposes in more positive ways.

A number of factors are converging, however, to force presidents to exert more influence over the way universities use the significant influence of athletics. First, the NCAA is holding presidents more accountable for the conduct of their athletic programs in matters relating to institutional control. Simply put, when they began getting fired for athletic department violations, institutional presidents began to take a more active role in athletic department affairs. Second, the virtual explosion of public interest in college athletics and the rapid proliferation of media coverage raised athletics' visibility to previously unimagined levels. This explosion of media attention, coupled with the growing need to market higher education to an increasingly skeptical public, suggests that presidents, and the academic community they represent, take a more active role in managing that exposure. Thus, the heretofore hands-off, keep-me-off-the-front-page approach to managing this powerful university resource no longer serves greater institutional purposes. In short, athletics' visibility and public influence must be looked upon as something not simply to be tolerated but rather harnessed and exploited for larger university gain.

REDEFINING INSTITUTIONAL RETURN ON INVESTMENT IN ATHLETICS

Currently, institutional return on investment (ROI) in athletics is measured in one way—whether the bottom of the income statement is black or red. While universities consider a few benefits that cannot be measured in hard dollars when determining the ROI of their athletic departments, consideration of athletics' entertainment value or its potential to unite various campus constituent groups is minimal. An athletic department that does

not operate in the black is invariably viewed by faculty and by many academic administrators as an unnecessary financial drain on the institution.

While academic deans assert that they too feel pressure to balance their
departmental budgets, the financial standard against which athletics is measured is far more stringent because athletic department activities are generally not looked upon as being directly connected to the central purpose of
the institution. Regardless of whether this assertion is valid, the academic
community usually views what transpires on a daily basis in the English or
chemistry departments as being more central to the academic mission of the
institution than what occurs in the athletic department. The result is a
greater tolerance for using general university funds to supplement the English or chemistry department operating budgets than to supplement the
athletic department budget.

To realize the New Standard, institutions can no longer afford to evaluate
their athletic department ROI solely on financial results. Such a change in
approach will break what amounts to a vicious cycle of short-term, economically driven athletic department decision making. It will free athletic departments to conduct their affairs within a framework of long-term student-
athlete welfare and institutional benefits. Currently, the pressure to balance
athletic department budgets results in an excessive drive to win-at-all-cost.
Such a drive results in decisions being made to maximize on-the-field or
court performance at the expense of the best long-term educational interests
of the institution and its student-athletes. Such pressure limits an athletic
department's potential for developing alternative methods through which it
can contribute to the mission and general goals of the institution. The end
result is that we remain shackled by a standard of measuring ROI only in
economic terms and on-the-field success.

Only when athletic departments are provided some relief from the pressure to operate in the black can they begin to invest in some of the fundamental changes suggested in this book. Less pressure to balance budgets
means less pressure to win-at-all-cost; less pressure to win-at-all-cost means
more room to make decisions based upon the academic and personal welfare
of the student-athlete and the broader good of the institution. Allowing
more consideration of student-athlete welfare, professional development,
institutional imaging, and community service initiatives, which will be
outlined in the following pages, will enable athletics to realize more fully its
potential to contribute to higher education's mission. The result is a greater
athletic department ROI as measured by the New Standard—not by a
financial bottom line.

This fundamental change in the way in which the institutional contribution of athletics is viewed is critical if higher education is to maximize its
ROI in athletics. While the result could be less actual dollars generated by

athletics, the overall ROI of a program that contributes to the mission of the university in a wide variety of ways will be far greater than one that balances its budget but becomes alienated in the process from the academic community. This alienation comes from having departmental goals that relate solely to on-the-field performance, entertainment appeal, and dollars generated. If provided the opportunity, directive, and support, athletic departments can produce significant institutional rewards that might not show up on a balance sheet but clearly increase institutional ROI in athletics. To achieve the New Standard, such a change in investment philosophy is critical.

ADDRESSING THE WIN-AT-ALL-COST MIND-SET

Higher education leaders must begin to address in earnest the pervading win-at-all-cost philosophy surrounding their athletic programs. This call for a de-emphasis in the importance of the final score is likely to be dismissed as unrealistic. Indeed, asking coaches, alumni, fans, and the media to consider that there is far more to college athletics than national rankings and victories over an arch rival is easy to reject as simply impossible. After all, winning is the "American Way." General George Patton, a great American hero, is credited with saying, "Americans love a winner and will not tolerate a loser." Yes, fans and alumni crave winning teams, and as a result it is easy to rationalize all the problems of college athletics by claiming that they are a result of "having to win or get fired." With such a mind-set, change is simply not possible. Or, is it?

In a 1990 poll conducted for the Knight Commission on Athletics by Louis Harris and Associates, Inc., university personnel were asked to choose one factor that *should* be the primary consideration of a big-time athletic program. Of those polled, 87 percent of the university presidents, 83 percent of trustees, 88 percent of athletic directors, 76 percent of faculty, and 93 percent of coaches indicated that "making sure student-athletes get an education" *should* be the top consideration. Even an overwhelming majority of the public surveyed (91 percent) believed in this goal. This was compared to 8 percent of presidents, 7 percent of trustees, 25 percent of athletic directors, and 33 percent of coaches who said that making sure student-athletes get an education *is* the primary goal of most big-time athletic programs (Louis Harris & Associates 1990). Apparently, most everyone involved in intercollegiate athletics agrees on what athletic programs and their coaches *should* be doing. The question is whether higher education leaders have the backbone to see that it gets done.

Undoubtedly, influencing a shift in our society's win-at-all-cost mind-set will be a difficult challenge. Even though most people, including the general public, agree that college athletics should be about more than winning games, it is all too easy to dismiss what "should be" for what "is." There is, however, an inherent flaw in this approach as it applies to higher education. Specifically, it involves the issue of whether those of us in higher education should *follow* public opinion or attempt to *lead* it.

Granted, educational leaders may not be in a position to address directly our society's obsession with winning. Nevertheless, that same society looks to higher education to provide educational leadership. Thus, higher education leaders have the right and the responsibility to address the issue of how our society's philosophy concerning winning applies to athletics conducted within an educational setting. In addition, higher education leaders clearly have the authority and responsibility to address the issue of how those who work within higher education are evaluated. These two points cannot be disputed. This is like an individual set of parents, who cannot have a direct impact on the unacceptably high rate of teenage smoking, but who certainly have the right and responsibility to address the issue directly with their own children.

Higher education leaders must address the win-at-all-cost philosophy that drives their athletic programs because this philosophy pervades not only college athletics but high school, junior high school, and grade school athletics as well. With the win-at-all-cost philosophy filtering down to these levels of sport, higher education has a responsibility to force national dialogue on the subject. Our highly visible college athletic programs offer the best vehicle through which this issue can be addressed. To that end, higher education leaders must stand up and declare that winning is not everything, particularly in an educational setting.

As emphasized earlier in this chapter, athletic departments must exist for more than simply providing entertainment and winning championship trophies. Their primary purpose must be to contribute to the academic mission of the institution in direct, timely, and meaningful ways. Only until this fundamental shift in ideology occurs will athletics be able to justify fully its place on campus. Without this shift, college athletics will, in time, lose its meaning. Championship banners fade, trophies tarnish, and money generated gets spent. What has lasting impact is education—as when student-athletes leave our programs to become positive contributors to society, as with coaches who are educators who positively influence our young people and have impact in fostering in our society an appreciation for, and support of, education at all levels.

Many people contend that influencing society is not the responsibility of our college athletic programs, that college athletics is simply entertainment with no larger purpose. While that point can be argued, there can be no debate over the responsibility of higher education leaders to provide leadership as it applies to the conduct of athletic programs that exist within educational systems. The programs we run and the priorities we exhibit at the college level have a tremendous effect on conduct and priorities of athletic programs at the high school and grade school levels. The visibility and public interest in athletics at these levels provides opportunities to positively impact broader educational goals. But our priorities must be clear: athletic programs must supplement rather than dominate the educational institution of which they are a part.

As part of a team, your primary responsibility is to the team, and that responsibility is to maximize your contribution to the team's efforts to achieve its goals. Athletic programs are a part of the higher education team. Thus, the primary responsibility of athletic department personnel is to the institution: To maximize the athletic department's potential to contribute to the institution's efforts to fulfill its mission. And it is the responsibility of those throughout the institution to make certain that this potential is realized.

Institutions of higher education can no longer afford to waste athletics' tremendous potential by continuing to judge the success of athletic departments simply upon championship banners hung from gymnasium rafters, entertainment produced, and revenue generated. The issues facing higher education and our society are simply too daunting to only expect, and thus allow, a potentially powerful educational tool to be evaluated on such narrow, and ultimately meaningless, criteria. Athletics must contribute to higher education's mission in more relevant and timely ways than simply conducting games. To achieve this goal, athletic department success must be evaluated using the New Standard.

References

Kramer, Roy. Phone interview, 17 July 1996.

Louis Harris & Associates. 1990. Survey conducted for The Knight Foundation Commission on Intercollegiate Athletics. New York: Louis Harris & Associates.

National Collegiate Athletic Association. 1996. *1996-97 NCAA Manual*. Overland Park, KS: NCAA.

Thelin, John R., and Lawrence L. Wiseman. 1989. *The Old College Try: Balancing Academics and Athletics in Higher Education*. Report No. 4. Washington, DC: School of Education and Human Development, The George Washington University, p. 3.

CHAPTER 2

Higher Education's Purpose

To Serve Society

From the beginning, the American college was cloaked with a public purpose, with a responsibility to the past, present and future.

Frederick Rudolph
The American College and University

I t is not enough for a coach to articulate to a basketball team's best scorer his or her responsibility to score points. The coach must also foster in that individual an understanding of the strengths, limitations, and overall goals of the team. For example, a team with less talent than its opponent will likely be defeated in a fast-paced, run-and-gun game. Only by slowing down the pace of the game will the overmatched team have a chance to win. Thus, the scorer must exercise patience in choosing opportunities to score. If scoring opportunities are not executed in a fashion that is conducive to the team's success, the player's efforts, while well intentioned, will work against the team's best interests. If the scorer does not consider how his or her role fits within the team's limitations, the team will lose. And, if the player does not adjust his or her game according to the team's strengths and weaknesses, it is the coach's responsibility to take that player out of the game.

College athletics is not an island but rather one component of a larger whole. To carry out its mission effectively, those in college athletics must understand the parameters within which they operate. Thus, any meaningful discussion of the issues facing college athletics or the future direction of college athletics cannot occur without an understanding of the history and mission of higher education.

This chapter offers a brief historical perspective of the evolution of American higher education, concentrating on its mission, purpose, and goals, and how those goals relate to an athletic program. There is also mention of issues confronting our society that at first glance may not appear to be related to a discussion of the mission of higher education. However, because higher education's most fundamental purpose is to address the problems facing our society, mentioning those challenges is essential to the question of how athletics can contribute to higher education's efforts to meet its goals. The chapter concludes with a brief discussion of an issue that is affecting higher education's ability to fulfill its mission—a decline of public trust.

SERVING THE NEEDS OF SOCIETY

From its origin as small communities of teachers and students, American higher education has held serving society to be part of its fundamental purpose. Most discussions regarding higher education's role eventually return to this purpose.

In 1825, for example, Harvard professor George Ticknor referred to Harvard College as "the oldest of our greater public schools," thus recognizing the obligations of Harvard as an instrument of the public will. President Charles Eliot, in his inaugural address in 1869, promised the community "a rich return of learning, poetry and piety. . . . It [would] foster the sense of public duty." Harvard, in other words, would not forget to serve (Rudolph 1990, 359).

On a more contemporary note, J. Wade Gilley offers the following description of higher education's purpose in *Thinking About American Higher Education: The 1990's and Beyond*:

> As the nation's primary arsenal in worldwide economic competition, America's colleges and universities face a formidable challenge. Higher education must continually cross and recross the boundaries between the ivory tower and the world of work, proving itself a full partner in bringing competitive new products to market. Colleges and universities must also excite young people about science and math, tackle the growing problem of illiteracy, and ensure that coming generations of Americans are capable of living and working in a multicultural global society. (Gilley 1991, 88)

While such a simple purpose may be appropriate for early American higher education, how can the mission of an enterprise as big and diverse as higher education be boiled down to one principle? There are, after all, more than

3,600 two- and four-year institutions of higher learning of all types and sizes in the United States (*Chronicle of Higher Education* 1994, p. 7), including private, public, religiously affiliated, urban, rural, residential, and commuter schools.

Clark Kerr, former president of the University of California, Berkeley, maintains that higher education has become so large that the word *university* is no longer an appropriate description for our institutions of higher learning. "Multiversity," says Kerr, better describes the size and scope of higher education. He explains as follows:

> The University of California last year had operating expenditures from all sources of nearly half a billion dollars, with almost another 100 million for construction; a total employment of over 40,000 people, more than IBM and in a far greater variety of endeavors; operations in over a hundred locations, counting campuses, experiment stations, agriculture and urban extension centers, and projects abroad involving more than fifty countries; nearly 10,000 courses in its catalogues; some form of contact with nearly every industry, nearly every level of government, nearly every person in its region. Vast amounts of expensive equipment were serviced and maintained. Over 4,000 babies were born in its hospitals. It is the world's largest purveyor of white mice. It will soon have the world's largest primate colony. It will soon also have 100,000 students—30,000 of them at the graduate level; yet much less than one third of its expenditures are directly related to teaching. It already has nearly 200,000 students in extension courses—including one out of every three lawyers and one out of every six doctors in the state. (Kerr 1982, 7-8)

One might expect that such growth and diversification of programs and activities would diffuse an institution's commitment to this central purpose of serving society. Not so. While the evolution of American higher education has certainly resulted in the development of what would seem to be various subpurposes, the vast majority of the activities in which higher education engages continue to relate in some way to serving the public will.

From teaching to encouraging economic development, from building a sense of community to being an agent of social change, the mission of higher education is many things to many people. With a 350-year history and such tremendous diversity, it is no wonder that higher education is looked upon to accomplish such a wide variety of tasks. While the founders of Harvard College could not, in their wildest imaginings, have envisioned the size and scope of the higher education enterprise of the 1990s, they could certainly appreciate the common purpose of their institution and that of modern-day universities. Although some may claim it simplistic, higher education's purpose today essentially remains what it was in 1633: to serve the public will by helping to meet the many problems, needs, and challenges that face society. The effectiveness with which higher education continues to respond to those needs will define it in the future.

In his work entitled *Higher Learning,* Derek Bok, president emeritus of Harvard University, identifies a key characteristic of the American system of higher education that, despite its continued growth and diversification, allows it to remain flexible and motivated to respond to the needs of society. Specifically, the degree to which "our colleges and universities compete with one another—for faculty, for students, for funds and even for successful athletics teams" enables American higher education to be responsive to public need (Bok 1986, 14). The resulting competition has long been encouraged through widely publicized rankings of colleges and universities. Not until recently have such rankings been prevalent in other countries. Thus, because of the competitive environment within which they operate, American universities must, as a matter of survival, be responsive to the needs of the public. Colleges and universities must be outward-looking and ever aware of changing social, scientific, and public trends.

Coaches and athletic administrators must understand and appreciate the historical roots of American higher education. Owing to the tremendous public interest in major college athletics—complete with its nightly television coverage, daily newspaper features, and stadiums full of adoring fans—it is easy for those who work in college athletics to think that the university revolves around the athletic program. Regardless of their athletic success or their public popularity, coaches and athletic administrators must respect the fact that athletics is simply one component of a huge enterprise, and further that higher education will survive with or without athletics. To think otherwise would be foolhardy. After all, American higher education was in existence for more than 200 years before the first intercollegiate athletic contest was held.

The fanfare around athletics tends to obfuscate the fact that athletics, to have any relevance within the educational community, must have a connection between its purpose and the purpose of higher education. It must become a fundamental expectation that athletic department personnel fully understand and appreciate higher education's primary purpose of serving the public. Ultimately, for athletics to be considered a viable, contributing member of the higher education community, it must be demonstrated that it contributes in a meaningful way to serving the public.

Further, athletic department personnel sometimes think their department deserves special treatment because athletics is the only department on campus that is engaged in a highly competitive undertaking; the reasoning is that such competitiveness makes them a unique component of the higher education team. While an athletic contest certainly provides a more immediate, clearer, and far more visible delineation between winner and loser, every department within a university is engaged in high-stakes competition. Jobs are on the line, as are large sums of money in the form of grants and various government and public appropriations. Competition amongst institutions for good students and top faculty is intense. So while athletics represents a competitive and highly visible activity, the institution is engaged in a much bigger game involving far bigger stakes.

The central challenge for all components of the higher education community is to demonstrate their utility. If a particular department does not meet a clear need and does not contribute to the central purpose of the institution, it will be eliminated. Similarly, if a university does not meet the public's needs sufficiently, students will no longer be drawn to it, donors will no longer make contributions, and the state will no longer help fund it. It will become obsolete. That being the case, athletic department personnel must meet this standard of utility as it applies to higher education's larger purpose.

Serving the needs of the public has meant different things at different times. The three primary vehicles through which higher education has served the public are teaching, research, and service. The emphasis on each of these categories varies over time, as does their relative importance from institution to institution. For example, many institutions continue to see the teaching function—which has its roots in colonial America—as their primary focus.

The following discussion briefly reviews the teaching, research, and service functions of higher education, and it links their emergence to the forces at work in society during various periods of our country's history. The discussion will demonstrate that American higher education is malleable and capable of adjusting as necessary to serve the ever-changing needs of an ever-changing society. The discussion will conclude by showing how the role of athletics must be linked with these three mission components to further the larger purpose of higher education.

TEACHING—THE FOUNDATION

American higher education began with Harvard and the Puritans. The Puritans who settled in Massachusetts, "although bigoted and intolerant of other religions, were committed to careful examination of their own beliefs. They detested 'ignorant sinners' for both reasons—ignorance and sin. They insisted upon educating their children and they considered a learned ministry vital to the community" (Westmeyer 1985, 8).

To that end, John Eliot proposed a college for Massachusetts Bay in a 1633 letter to the General Court, the colonial legislature. On 28 October 1636, the Massachusetts General Court passed the legislative act that led to the founding of Harvard College. Classes began in 1638. The establishment of Harvard and the early colonial colleges that followed would "train the schoolmasters, the divines, the rulers, the cultural ornaments of society—the men who would spell the difference between civilization and barbarism. . . . [O]f course, a religious commonwealth required educated clergy, but it also needed leaders disciplined by knowledge and learning, it needed followers disciplined by leaders, it needed order" (Rudolph 1990, 6-7).

The early colonies were viewed simply as extensions of England. Thus, the early colonial colleges were closely modeled after the Old World colleges of Cambridge and Oxford in England. The English system of education centered on general education in philosophy, religion, and values, which was a holistic approach to educating and developing the character of clergy and aristocracy for leadership positions. In the view of the colonies' religious and civic leaders, this approach to education was necessary to "civilize" the New World by molding it with Old World principles. This philosophical approach to American higher education prevailed virtually unchallenged for more than a hundred years.

This commitment to the development of our country's human resources has been higher education's most central and enduring focus. That being the case, the fundamental tenet of any discussion of athletics' role in higher education must relate to its educational and developmental impact on student participants. The perception that athletic departments have abdicated their responsibility as it relates to the educational and personal development of student-athletes has led to widespread cynicism regarding the role of athletics in higher education. Thus, this commitment to the "holistic" development of student-athletes—academic and personal, rather than simply athletic—must drive athletic department decision making.

RESEARCH—MEETING PRACTICAL NEEDS

With the approach of the American Revolution in the 1760s, the colonies' relationship to England began to change. A yearning for independence began to stir in the New World. The seeds of the American Revolution were being planted. Some of those changes were being played out in American higher education. In New York and Philadelphia, Kings College and the College of Philadelphia were embarking on a new path for higher education, one that sought to meet the needs not of a colonial society but rather an emerging American society.

In 1754, Kings College announced that its course of study would emphasize surveying, navigation, geography, history, and natural philosophy. This course of study was designed to meet the practical rather than the philosophical or religious needs of the emerging and rapidly expanding New World. Although the college's success was limited, it served to set the stage for the College of Philadelphia in 1756, which established, under the leadership of Scotsman William Smith and with the support of Benjamin Franklin, a three-year course of study that placed significant emphasis on subjects that served more practical purposes.

This shift in curricular emphasis continued, and by the mid-1800s, the traditional English approach to higher education was being challenged by a different model. The German or "scientific" view of the university differed from the English view in that it was based not upon the teaching of traditional knowledge but rather upon the acquisition of new knowledge.

> The German system was based on the notion that institutions of higher education should be workshops of free scientific research . . . unlike the "cultural school," which declared the universal validity of one verities (truth). The "German scientific school" did not suppose any such value. The significance of a truth or a fact had to be demonstrated through rational, experienced techniques. Whereas the cultural thought valued by the upper class served as the grist of the subject matter in the cultural school, the scientific model declared that although there might be one truth, such truth had to stand on its own under scientific scrutiny without any ties to social class. (Chu, Segrave, and Becker 1985, 39)

Educational leaders began to incorporate principles of the German approach into the American model of higher education. To see what prompted this change, one only has to consider where the country was in its growth and development; what had served the country for the previous two centuries was not what would serve it best in the future. The United States changed rapidly in the second half of the nineteenth century. The country, like a young colt that has finally found its legs and bearings, was galloping rapidly westward, growing and maturing as it went. A sense of unlimited horizons, prosperity, and accomplishment gripped its citizens. New territories were being settled; railroads were being built; fortunes were being made. There was opportunity for all. The Industrial Revolution was in full swing. It was a new day pointing to a new future, and the United States was rushing headlong into it.

> Everywhere the states were throwing away old constitutions, writing new ones more acceptable to the age. A country that was hurrying into the future required colleges that would hurry along with it. The

American colleges would, therefore, experience the same challenge as political parties, state constitutions and economic institutions. They would be asked to pass the test of utility. They would have to answer to the question of whether they were serving the needs of a people whose interest in yesterday hardly existed, and whose interest in today was remarkably limited to its usefulness for getting to tomorrow. (Rudolph 1990, 110)

With such unlimited possibilities, what was needed from higher education was not more philosophers or seekers of truth but technological and agricultural research and development. Land had to be cleared and farmed. Railroads needed to be built, steel manufactured, frontier towns and cities raised. If higher education was to respond to the rapidly changing demands of the American public, it would be necessary to incorporate into its system programs and a philosophy that would result in the development of practical and useful knowledge and discoveries for a country that was galloping into the future.

While the parallel between higher education's teaching function and athletics is clear, the significance of the research function and its relevance to athletics is less apparent, though nonetheless important. Although higher education's primary purpose of serving the needs of society has remained constant, the way in which it has met that purpose has undergone significant changes. Serving the public has meant different things at different times. Higher education has exhibited an ability not only to perceive such changing needs, but, more important, to respond to them accordingly. College athletic leaders would be well served by taking note of higher education's ability to adjust its philosophy and programs to meet changing societal needs and thus to fulfill its larger purpose. More specifically, coaches and athletic administrators must be aware of the rapidly changing needs of higher education and how their programs can be altered to meet those needs more effectively.

To be a viable contributing member of the higher education team, the athletic community must continually assess the relevance of its purpose and the effectiveness with which it is meeting its stated goals; the community must evaluate whether it is meeting its full potential to contribute to higher education's mission. Unfortunately, many coaches and athletic administrators continue to resist efforts to assess critically athletics' role in higher education. If higher education, an enterprise significantly larger and older than college athletics, is flexible enough to change to meet emerging public need, athletics should demonstrate similar flexibility.

SERVICE—GETTING INVOLVED WITH THE COMMUNITY

Just as teaching and research developed as the product of society's needs, so did the ideal of service. Service activities such as community outreach, volunteer work, and faculty consulting are one element of "serving the needs of society." "While the German and English models of higher education vied for dominance, they were both affected by the emergence of an American view that higher education could not be separated from the needs of the people. 'Application' was the key word. How could education serve the practical needs of the people?" (Chu, Segrave, and Becker 1985, 40).

In the early 1900s, a spirit of "progressivism" swept through the United States. Progressivism was a belief that individuals had an obligation to give something back to society—to help society become not just bigger, but better and more just. During this time, the labor movement emerged as a major force in the country. Theodore Roosevelt initiated his Square Deal. The emergence of American Progressivism corresponded with the emergence of land grant universities designed to meet the needs of their states; these two trends led to an increased attention to service as a major purpose of higher education.

> The Wisconsin Idea, as this program of university service was called, rested on the conviction that informed intelligence when applied to the problems of modern society could make democracy work more effectively. Hostile to pecuniary values, charged with more than a touch of moral righteousness, the Wisconsin Idea placed the people's university at the service of the people, sought to protect them from the greed, privilege and corrupting power of great wealth, and made of the university a kind of teacher-counselor-companion to the people at large. In varying degrees other state universities revealed the same spirit, but none came as close as the University of Wisconsin in epitomizing the spirit of Progressivism and the service ideal. (Rudolph 1990, 363)

The parallel between higher education's service component and athletics is direct and thus an area where athletics can be used to meet higher education's purpose in powerful ways. Of all the components of higher education, athletics is in the best position to contribute in the area of service, for it has the resources to make a difference: television exposure, tremendously talented coaches and student-athletes, and a society that idolizes athletes. These resources must not be wasted. Leaders in athletics and in higher education must insist that athletic programs increase their efforts in addressing broader social issues through community service initiatives.

CHALLENGES FACING SOCIETY

One has only to pick up a newspaper to gain a sense of the challenges facing our society. Deficiencies in public education affect everything from illiteracy rates to our ability to compete in a global economy. Other broad issues facing our country are the disintegration of the family, the challenges of living in an increasingly diverse and technologically advanced society, and environmental degradation. Crime, poverty, and calls to restore in our young people a strong sense of ethical awareness and civic responsibility are additional concerns that must be addressed. These problems are enormous, and our society is facing them in an environment of declining resources and increasing costs.

Faced with such daunting challenges, the need for higher education to become actively and aggressively engaged with the issues of the day has become particularly critical. Robert Atwell, former president of the American Council on Education (ACE), offered these thoughts on the role that higher education should play in addressing such challenges.

> Given the resources it has invested in higher education, society needs to harness the intellectual horsepower available principally in colleges and universities to deal with the many manifestations of our current social deficit. In fact, it is difficult to imagine a problem confronting society, from the state of public education to the need for better health care to environmental degradation, that colleges and universities could not or should not play a big part in solving. This is not a role that higher education should embrace reluctantly, but one toward which it should aspire. (Wingspread 1993, 53)

If the challenge of responding to the many problems facing our society is not enough, higher education must confront these issues while facing a significant decline in public trust. According to a 1995 Louis Harris & Associates poll, only 27 percent of Americans had "a great deal of confidence" in the leaders of higher education, down from 61 percent in 1966.

Exorbitant tuition increases, research overcharges, athletic scandals, coaches being paid more than college presidents, ineffective teaching, and a general attitude of arrogance have all contributed to the public's loss of faith in higher education's ability to meet societal needs. Given that higher education's purpose is to help solve societal problems, the perception that higher education is not meeting those needs is particularly damning.

To gain a sense of the seriousness of this decline in trust, one need only consider the lead paragraph in a 1993 report on the future of American higher education entitled *An American Imperative: Higher Expectations for Higher Education*. Sponsored by The Johnson Foundation, the report was compiled by the Wingspread Group on Higher Education, a body of 16 leading educators, business leaders, and foundation executives. "A disturbing and dangerous mismatch exists," the report began, "between what American society needs of higher education and what it is receiving. Nowhere is the mismatch more dangerous than in the quality of undergraduate preparation provided on many campuses. The American imperative for the 21st century is that society must hold higher education to much higher expectations or risk national decline" (Wingspread 1993, 1).

As higher education's most visible resource, athletic programs are the primary means by which the public forms its perceptions regarding the quality, effectiveness, and purpose of our institutions of higher education. Therefore, athletic leaders must understand the effect that public trust in higher education has on its ability to address effectively the challenges before it; they also must understand athletics' tremendous influence on that public trust. If college athletics does not use its great societal influence responsibly, with the broader educational purposes of higher education in mind, it will lose its meaning. Before a strong, positive link can be forged between the purposes of athletics and higher education, athletic personnel must understand clearly the broad issues facing society and higher education. Without an awareness of these challenges and the absolutely vital role that higher education can play in addressing them, athletic programs can contribute in only superficial ways to higher education's purpose.

We must understand that athletics, while highly visible, is simply one component of a larger whole. As part of the higher education team, athletics has a responsibility not only to understand and embrace the goals and purpose of the team but also to contribute to those goals in meaningful ways.

Just as a business will downsize or eliminate a department that is no longer contributing in meaningful ways to the company's broad goals, so too will higher education. If athletics loses its relevance within the higher education setting, it will be discarded, and higher education will continue to survive. In the final analysis, higher education will structure itself according to what will enable it to meet effectively the most critical needs of the society it serves.

Those are the goals of our team. We must accept them and adjust our game accordingly.

References

Bok, Derek. 1986. *Higher Learning.* Cambridge, MA: Harvard University Press.
The Chronicle of Higher Education: The Almanac Issue, September 1, 1994, p. 7.
Chu, Donald, Jeffrey Segrave, and Beverly Becker. 1985. *Sport and Higher Education.* Champaign, IL: Human Kinetics Publishers.
Gilley, J. Wade. 1991. *Thinking about American Higher Education: The 1990's and Beyond.* New York: Macmillan/The American Council on Education.

Kerr, Clark. 1982. *The Uses of the University.* Cambridge, MA: Harvard University Press.

Louis Harris & Associates. 1995. *The Harris Poll, No. 17.* New York: Louis Harris & Associates.

Rudolph, Frederick. 1990. *The American College and University: A History.* Athens, GA: University of Georgia Press.

Westmeyer, Paul. 1985. *A History of American Higher Education.* Springfield, IL: Charles C. Thomas.

Wingspread Group on Higher Education. 1993. *An American Imperative: Higher Expectations for Higher Education.* Racine, WI: The Johnson Foundation.

CHAPTER 3

The Role of Athletics in Higher Education

As the programs of an organization reveal something about the nature of the organization, the sports of a school tell us something about the character of the social institution of higher education in America. Our colleges and universities have developed into a form unique among the world's places of higher learning. The presence of sport as a formal part of the school attests to this fact. How those sport programs are run, the behaviors that are tolerated or demanded, and the problems which remain unsolved tell us something of the nature of higher education and the American society on which it is dependent.

Donald Chu, Jeffrey Segrave, and Beverly Becker
Sport and Higher Education

Given intercollegiate athletics' popularity, one might assume that competitive sports have always been a part of higher education. But American higher education was in existence for more than 200 years before the first intercollegiate athletic contest (a boat race between the teams of Harvard and Yale in 1852) and more than 230 years before Rutgers and Princeton squared off in the first intercollegiate football contest.

Early American higher education was deeply rooted in religious principles. To the leaders of the colonial colleges, education was based upon rigorous study of the classics and devotion to God, which left no time for "games." Unproductive physical exercise of the sort suggested by an out-door gymnasium was unnecessarily trivial. According to Rudolph, "most college students in the early Nineteenth Century were drawn from farms where they had been trained to work but not to play. Young men did not need to be reminded that Americans judged their neighbors by their industry, not by their capacity for enjoyment" (Rudolph 1990, 152).

Cornell President Andrew White's response in 1873 to a challenge from 30 players from the University of Michigan to arrange a football game in Cleveland serves to illustrate how little value intercollegiate athletics was thought to add to a university's mission. "I will not permit thirty men to travel four hundred miles merely to agitate a bag of wind," he told them (in Rudolph 1990, 373). (Undoubtedly, President White's rest is disturbed at the spectacle of a modern-day football game between Michigan and Ohio State.)

How could something that as recently as the late nineteenth century was widely viewed as anti-intellectual, frivolous, and inconsequential evolve into higher education's most visible and, according to some, most impor-tant activity? This chapter will focus on that question. Rather than offering a strict historical treatment of the evolution of athletics within American higher education, however, its focus will be more narrowly upon athletics' role in higher education. This distinction between athletics' history and its role is significant. Just as it is important to distinguish between what those in athletics *do* (conduct games) versus what they are *about* (education) to fully realize athletics' potential to contribute to higher education's mission, it is far more important to understand and appreciate athletics' role within higher education than the specific dates, games, and personalities that comprise a strict historical treatment of the subject.

AN OPEN CHARTER

Although based upon the English and German systems of higher educa-tion, American higher education remained open and flexible regarding the incorporation of activities that uniquely served American society. And why not? In a new country with virtually unlimited potential, why limit the scope, reach, and potential of the very institution that held serving that society as its fundamental mission? Why not embrace athletics as part of the campus culture?

> Certainly, much of the reason for the claim of athletic responsibility by college leadership has been under pressure from the need for financial and student support. For the bulk of schools about the turn of the century, the need to attract money and students was vital. Most fundamental, however, was the openness of American conceptions of

the "charter" of higher education, that is, its proper goals and functions. With no traditionally accepted understanding of the methods
and objectives appropriate for American colleges and universities,
there was an openness of the "charter" definition that permitted the
inclusion of radically different programs within American higher education. (Chu 1989, 35-36)

By the late 1800s, attitudes against the involvement of students in
athletic activities began to soften. Students, being young and energetic,
came to feel that a little frivolity was not such a bad thing. Regardless of
whether the university establishment approved, students liked athletics,
and, more significantly, so did the public, especially football. "In 1893 New
York was thrown into a virtual frenzy by the annual Thanksgiving game
between Yale and Princeton. Hotels were jammed. On Fifth Avenue blue
and white Yale banners hung from the Vanderbilt and Whitney mansions.
The Sloanes, the Alexanders, and the Scribners displayed the colors of Old
Nassau. Clergymen cut short their Thanksgiving Day services in order to
get off to the game in time. Clearly, football had arrived" (Rudolph 1990,
375).

Up to this point, university athletic activities were operated by student-
run associations. Students were responsible for arranging travel, securing
equipment, and the general administration of the athletic program. Athletics was simply an institutional afterthought, an activity to keep students
amused, but certainly not critical to the educational mission of the university. That outlook was soon to change. Due to the rapidly growing public
interest in athletics and the resultant capability to generate revenue,
college administrators became more curious about athletics' potential to
benefit the institution in a broader sense. As it became apparent that public
interest in college athletics was not going to subside, universities began to
consider athletics' formal incorporation into the mission, structure, and
culture of their institutions. College athletics at the turn of the century was
becoming too important to remain a student-run enterprise. Thus, institutions throughout the country were coming to the conclusion that such a
visible program required a more appropriate level of institutional oversight.
While some hailed the decision, others referred to it as the unleashing of "a
monster" within the gates of higher education (Rudolph 1990, 155).

FORMAL INCORPORATION OF ATHLETICS INTO HIGHER EDUCATION

While athletics' visibility and its capacity to keep students amused were
important, the ever-constant search for financial resources made athletics
especially attractive to presidents and trustees.

> While the need for resources has remained an ever-pressing imperative throughout the history of higher education in this country, it was only at the turn of the century, with the invention of mass sports in America and the complex of factors that affected the university's internal and external constituencies, that resource acquisition through athletics became a possibility. A sports-hungry populace consumed athletic entertainment with increasing gusto as the tempo of industrialization, urbanization, leisure time, and accumulation of expendable capital quickened. The large land-grant schools saw a means of acquiring increased support from the legislature and the people. (Chu 1989, 33-34)

Regardless of whether a successful sports team generated additional resources and political favor for a university—points that remain in dispute to this day—college presidents *believed* that a successful football program legitimized their institution as a major, big-time university. This trend intensified during the 1930s when transportation and communications advancements made long-distance travel and the broadcast of games on the radio a part of an expanding sports marketplace. Intercollegiate athletics was no longer regional in scope. With these changes came opportunity to gain widespread national prestige and visibility. Athletics was formally incorporated into higher education's structure because academic leaders believed that a successful athletic team could serve an important public-relations function for the university, which in turn would result in increased financial support.

> To build a major university, certain structures were necessary—a board of trustees, faculty of various rank, a president, departments organized by discipline, department heads, and an athletic stadium. Thus, a sports program became both the institutional rule and a means of engendering an institutional myth. As the Harvard Man came to symbolize the distinctiveness of that institution, so too did Frank Merriwell of Yale and the Fightin' Irish of Notre Dame, come to represent the qualities of all from those schools. (Chu 1989, 45)

Enhancing an institution's visibility and increasing its potential to acquire resources were not the only benefits of a successful athletic program. Athletic teams also served a unifying function for the university community. With student enrollment increasing and becoming more geographically and ethnically diverse, what heretofore was considered a college "family" was becoming more fractured. By 1900, students no longer studied the same groups of predetermined courses, for the elective system of course selection was beginning to transform institutional curricula. Faculty were engaged in a wide variety of research. Alumni were spread far and wide. Universities were in need of something that could bind these various groups together in pursuit of a common purpose. Athletics provided that focus. A successful athletic team offered a common activity that an increasingly fragmented university community could rally around, thereby promoting the "old college spirit." Athletics, it was said, would bring the family together.

> Whether it be Kansas, Nebraska, Oklahoma, or Texas, in football or basketball, the fortunes of college sport teams are followed avidly. As a cynical friend of Ohio State President Harold Enarson once remarked, "Now that public hangings are forbidden, where else can you go and enjoy the contagion of the crowd and its excitement?" (Enarson 1980, 23)

> Intercollegiate athletics draws people together—to care for a common purpose in an atmosphere of exhilaration. With few tangible means of evaluating institutional or regional quality, the exploits of sports teams serve as quality indicators visible to all. (Chu 1989, 159-60)

When higher education leaders were moving to incorporate athletics into the academe, little mention was made of the supposed personal and character development benefits associated with athletic participation. While institutional oversight was deemed crucial for purposes of managing the revenues and visibility generated by athletics, academic leaders apparently did not deem such supposed educational by-products of athletic participation worthy of their supervision. But of this, more later.

By the 1920s, collegiate sports had fully captured the public's interest. To keep up with this interest, universities began to pump money into athletic programs, especially in the building of huge stadiums. "Public craving for sports, the cultivation of heroes and their teams, and the dynamism of the 1920s and 1930s, all spoke for a less insulated campus and one more responsive to the public's needs" (Chu 1989, 56). College sports were clearly becoming a big-business operation with big stadiums, big-name coaches, coast-to-coast travel, and national radio broadcasts. The student-run athletic team had given way to professional coaches, big stadiums, intense media attention, and an increased emphasis on winning. This shift in emphasis was justified by a reassuring sense that by providing programs to satiate the public's desire for entertainment through sports, colleges and universities were providing a public service and meeting, as was their purpose, a public need. But such growth had its price.

> From football as public relations to football as business would not, at some institutions, be much of a distance. Obviously what enhanced both the publicity and business dimensions of football was the degree to which it became a game not for the players but for the spectators. Any chance of the game ever again being played for fun by college under-

graduates was perhaps lost in 1915 when the University of Pittsburgh, in order to spur the sale of programs at football games, introduced the soon widely copied custom of plastering large numerals on the players' backs. There was something tragically symbolic about that 1915 gesture at the University of Pittsburgh, for it suggested the degree to which the game had fallen beyond the control of those who played it, the degree to which it now belonged to the paying customers and to the treasurer of the athletic association. (Rudolph 1990, p. 386)

With the shift from student-run, participation-based sport for exercise and amusement to sport for visibility, revenue generation, and spectator interest, college athletics moved from an activity that was internally controlled for internal purposes to an activity that had the entertainment of external constituents as its purpose.

An early effort to highlight such concern was a report issued in 1929 by the Carnegie Foundation entitled *American College Athletics*. The following passage illustrates the tone of that report, which up to that time was the most comprehensive analysis of the state of college athletics.

The management of athletics, both intercollegiate and intramural, entails an appointment of valid responsibilities, few of which are at present borne by undergraduates. Now, the bearing of responsibilities presents one of the most important means by which youth may be matured into manhood and certain qualities that are desirable in any citizen may be developed and strengthened. Yet, for one reason or another—the large amounts of money received or expended, the fear lest habits of study may be impaired, or a general feeling that young men of college age are not old enough for the tasks involved—more and more of the responsibilities that athletics imply have been progressively shifted from younger shoulders to older. . . . Much of the genuine educational benefit that responsibility in the administrative control of college athletics might bring is reaped today by men whose formal education has ended. (Savage 1929, 102-103)

On a more contemporary note, Wilford Bailey and Taylor Littleton, in their 1991 book *Athletics and Academe: An Anatomy of Abuses and a Prescription for Reform*, cite this shift in focus as the fundamental cause of virtually all athletic abuses. The authors argue that athletics' compromising of academic and institutional integrity is systemic; it results from athletics' inherent separation from the academic community and ethics of the university—this coupled with the lack of leadership to fight it. They explain that with a primary purpose of providing entertainment, athletics is more a property of the public than of the university. With the decision to entertain comes an inherent commitment to cater to the consumer rather than student-athletes, faculty, or other members of the university community. This tendency has only increased with television. Further, they explain, American television/entertainment culture has as its foundation a pattern of production, consumption, and marketing of services and is a far cry from higher education's roots in teaching, service, and a search for truth. The result is the loss of any meaningful institutional control over athletic programs, which creates a relationship that is not simply uncomfortable but represents a sharply divided double culture.

Many contend that this change in the nature of collegiate sports cheapened the university and compromised the entire educational system. Others say that the evolution of intercollegiate athletics into a huge business enterprise was simply inevitable.

> It is perhaps unfair to attribute to the college president sole responsibility for the formal incorporation of sport within American higher education. Acting within the milieu of a weak charter and lack of guaranteed funding and other resources, and subject to the beguiling temptations of business attitudes and philosophies, the college president may have been merely the agent through which otherwise inevitable incidents were enacted. (Chu 1989, 48)

JUSTIFYING ATHLETICS' PLACE ON CAMPUS

Any company or organization must have a clear purpose and meet an identifiable need. "All organizations require this acceptance (of legitimacy). They seek a strong charter from society, which is acquired largely by statements of organizational purpose (how does the organization fulfill societal needs?) and by demonstration of rationality in its process and programs" (Chu 1989, 62).

In higher education's case, the need to justify how it contributes to the betterment of society is particularly acute because it depends upon so many external constituent groups for support. Students, the public, state legislators, and faculty all stake a claim to higher education's purpose. The appropriation of a significant amount of taxpayer dollars to campuses and students across the country intensifies the need for academic leaders to articulate clearly and realize fully higher education's purpose.

When a company seeks to diversify by offering a new service, it must be clear as to how the addition of that service will contribute to its profitability and purpose. Similarly, when a university considers adding a new department or field of study, it must be clear about how that new department will contribute to the mission of the institution. While its visibility and potential to generate revenue was reason enough to open the door to athletics' initial incorporation into the higher education enterprise, there was also a need to justify its purpose from an educational standpoint.

> Response to this need to rationalize the newly claimed athletic enterprise centered around claims that intercollegiate sport not only aided the economic prosperity of the college but that it also had educational benefits for the individual athletes. If athletics could be demonstrated to be a learning enterprise, or at least one which provided the capital necessary for the work of the college, then domain consensus might be achieved. If alumni, legislators, and the public could be given winning sport teams, while educational critics and the faculty accepted that athletics aided the brick and mortar as well as the character-building concerns of education, then acquisition of the resources of money, students, and internal support might be possible. (Chu 1989, 65)

Therefore, it was argued that participation in athletics supplemented the educational process because lessons that could not be learned from a textbook could be learned on the playing fields. Sports could be used as a vehicle to instill in participants an appreciation for concepts such as teamwork, discipline, and perseverance, which directly related to the teaching component of higher education's mission. The claim that coaches were teachers and educators served to solidify further the link between athletics and education. The assertion that participation in athletics was educational in that it helped build the character of those involved was perpetuated by coaches and athletic administrators and embraced by higher education leaders, state politicians, the public, and most of the media, faculty, and students.

In spite of such high-minded claims regarding its potential to contribute to the academic and personal welfare of participants, athletics' initial incorporation into higher education had to do with generating money, visibility, and prestige for the university. Had the public and media not taken such an interest in college athletics in the 1890s, it might still be an intramural rather than intercollegiate activity. Simply put, when university presidents recognized that alumni would donate money to develop and support programs, athletics quickly became institutionalized. Colleges needed resources of all kinds to advance their mission. A successful sports program had the potential to generate revenue, visibility, and prestige for the university—all resources that could well serve university needs.

Thus, the following three major justifications for university-sponsored intercollegiate athletics were identified, refined, and promoted:

1. Athletics generates revenue, visibility, and prestige for the university.
2. Athletics provides entertainment and serves a unifying function for an increasingly fragmented university community.

3. Athletics is educational (character building) for the students participating.

Educating and building character in participants; generating revenue, visibility, and prestige for the institution; and unifying the college community are all worthy goals. Even so, the question needs to be raised as to whether they continue to have relevance in a world that has changed markedly in the last century. We must ask whether these goals continue to apply in the 1990s and, if so, whether the athletic community is successfully achieving these goals. If athletic programs are not delivering results on what are alleged to be their primary functions, what can be done to ensure that they do? And most significant of all, if it is determined that collegiate athletics cannot meet these objectives, should such programs continue to be sponsored by colleges and universities in their present form? These are the questions facing educational leaders as they consider athletics' role in higher education during the next decades. We will explore these same questions in the chapters that follow.

References

Bailey, Wilford, and Taylor Littleton. 1991. *Athletics and Academe: An Anatomy of Abuses and a Prescription for Reform.* New York: Macmillan/American Council on Education.

Chu, Donald. 1989. *The Character of American Higher Education and Intercollegiate Sport.* Albany, NY: State University of New York Press.

Chu, Donald, Jeffrey Segrave, and Beverly Becker. 1985. *Sport and Higher Education.* Champaign, IL: Human Kinetics Publishers.

Enarson, Harold L. "Collegiate Athletics: Views from the Front Office." *Educational Record* 61(4), (Fall, 1980): 22–31.

Rudolph, Frederick. 1990. *The American College and University: A History.* Athens, GA: University of Georgia Press.

Savage, Howard J., et al., 1929. *American College Athletics.* New York: Carnegie Foundation.

CHAPTER 4

Is Athletics Meeting Its Purpose?

There is a common belief in the value of sport, which we have chosen to view as a myth not because it is untrue, but because it is generally accepted without question. If this common understanding, this myth about sport, is valid, it ought to withstand scrutiny. If it is not valid, we tax-paying citizens who make decisions about the future of our educational system need to know. . . . If sport does live up to the myth surrounding it, even if only in part, perhaps we should invest more heavily in sports. For example, we could make room for all students in sport, not just the athletically superior. On the other hand, what if it were demonstrated scientifically that most or all of the myths about school sport have no empirical basis, that there are no data to support them, no evidence of positive effects? As a taxpayer, parent, educator, or concerned citizen, what would your response be? What should it be?

Andrew Miracle and C. Roger Rees
Lessons of the Locker Room

It is perhaps axiomatic that challenges to any system are scorned by those fully vested in the system. On the other hand, organizations that do not continually reevaluate their goals and their effectiveness in meeting those goals will eventually become obsolete. Critical analysis of college athletics is particularly important because a fundamental purpose of higher education is to encourage critical thinking by challenging pre-existing assumptions in an effort to seek truth. Therefore, the college athletic community should not fear, resist, or ignore such scrutiny; rather, it should welcome the chance to rethink its purpose. Those who criticize college athletics should not be dismissed as simply destructive, particularly if the criticism is well formulated with suggestions for improvement.

Thus, the debate regarding whether athletics is meeting its stated purposes should not center on whether these questions should be asked, but rather on how athletics' contribution to higher education can be maximized. The credibility of any individual or organization depends upon whether the individual or organization does what it says it will. With both academe and the public questioning the role of athletics in higher education, critical debate regarding the effectiveness with which athletics accomplishes its goals should be encouraged. The following sections are intended to facilitate creative debate.

DOES ATHLETICS BUILD CHARACTER?

> Sports is a vital character builder. It molds the youth of our country for their roles as custodians of the republic. It teaches them to be strong enough to know they are weak and brave enough to face themselves when they are afraid. It teaches them to be proud and unbending in honest defeat, but humble and gentle in victory. . . . It gives them a predominance of courage over timidity, of appetite for adventure over loss of ease. (General Douglas MacArthur in Chu 1989, 65)

> For the past 8 years, we have been studying the effects of competition on personality. Our research began with the counseling of problem athletes, but it soon expanded to include athletes from every sport, at every level, from the high school gym to the professional arena. On the evidence gathered in this study, we can make some broad-range value judgments. We found no empirical support for the tradition that sport builds character. Indeed, there is evidence that athletic competition limits growth in some areas. It seems that the personality of the ideal athlete is not the result of any molding process, but comes out of the ruthless selection process that occurs at all levels of sport. Athletic competition has no more beneficial effects than intense endeavor in any other field. (Oglive and Tutko 1985, 268-269)

The claim that "sports builds character" has long been a widely held assumption in the United States. This largely unquestioned belief made the sponsorship of athletic programs seem logical, not only in colleges and universities but in high schools and junior highs as well. While the lessons learned in classrooms and laboratories in English and science were important, so, it seemed, were the lessons in discipline, teamwork, and perseverance taught on the playing fields. Although thousands of former and current student-athletes will swear by the value of competitive athletics, many others look back on their intercollegiate athletic experience with bitterness and regret.

Just as I was exposed to coaches who had a tremendously positive effect on my life, I was also subject to other coaches who had no interest in my personal or academic development or in that of any of my teammates. So from my experience, while there are lessons that participation in competitive athletics teaches, there were some practices that would be hard to defend from an educational standpoint. And as the money, television exposure, and pressure to win have increased, so too have practices that would be questionable in any educational setting.

Many groups have a vested interest in promoting the principle that participation in sport is a character-building activity. To justify their place in the educational community, coaches and athletic administrators must demonstrate that sports have educational value. The widespread acceptance of the educational value of athletics secures their power and status not only in the educational community but also in the public eye.

The justification that "sports build character" serves those in the athletic establishment in another important way. An unquestioned acceptance of this ideal relieves coaches of having to be accountable for teaching in a responsible manner. A coach can justify punishing an "undisciplined" student-athlete, running a few "bad apples" off the team and out of a scholarship, or verbally abusing a student-athlete by simply stating that he or she is "teaching life lessons." Thus, teaching methods deemed unacceptable for the classroom can be justified on the playing fields in the name of "building character."

Coaches and administrators are not alone in having an interest in promoting the "sports build character" ideal. The media, bowl representatives, television executives, and others who make a living off big-time athletics all have a stake in promulgating this belief. If it were determined that participation in major college athletics had no positive educational benefits, athletics' place on the college campus would be difficult to justify. If universities no longer sponsored athletics, coaches and administrators would no longer have jobs, at least not the same jobs. For this reason, the entire athletic community has a tremendous vested interest in promoting the "sports build character" ideal, regardless of its validity.

Not everyone has accepted without question the claim that participation in sports has significant educational benefits. Skepticism regarding the supposed benefits of athletic participation has almost been as much a part of the culture of sport as the increased heart rate and the sweat-soaked brow. In fact, the sentiment of higher education leaders that athletics was a frivolous activity prevented it from being sponsored as a university-sanctioned activity before the late nineteenth century. When it was formally incorporated into higher education, debate regarding athletics' value and place on campus intensified.

While athletics' role was debated on individual campuses for years, the issue was first raised as a national concern with the release of the Carnegie Foundation Study of American college athletics in 1929. The report addressed many concerns, including whether athletic participation had substantial educational value and whether all the attention and expense showered upon college athletic programs were justified. The report stated the following:

> To the development of the individual capacities of young men and women, their appreciation of true values, their powers of decision and choice, their sense of responsibility, and their ability to sustain it when once it comes to them—to the development of these and of all other best habits of mind and traits of character, college athletics must contribute far more than they have in the past if they are to justify the time and effort that are lavished upon them. (Savage 1929, 133-34)

Perhaps the most interesting aspect of the report was its analysis of the coach. It called into question coaches' propensity to make virtually every decision related to the game and the program themselves, leaving little opportunity for the students to develop their decision-making skills.

> The exigencies of the game forbid original thinking. Not many coaches understand what it means to let their men work out their own plays and conduct their own teams accordingly. It is a commonplace of adverse criticism of present-day coaching methods that many coaches tend to occupy too much of their men's time with fundamentals, too little with playing the game under conditions of contest. Yet, if athletics are to be "educational," the player must be taught to do his own thinking. In every branch of athletics the strategy of the game should not be beyond the capacity of the alertly-minded undergraduate. As matters now stand, no branch owes even a vestige of its strategy to the undergraduates engaged. Such matters are the affair of the coach. (Savage 1929, 176)

While the Carnegie report generated discussion, it did not result in much change. The lack of response, however, did not mean that such concerns would disappear. Since the publication of the Carnegie report, empirical data has continued to mount, indicating that the educational value of participation in intercollegiate athletics may have been greatly overemphasized. Some researchers even charge that participation in highly competitive athletics might actually hinder or arrest the development of various positive character traits.

A NARROWER WORLD VIEW

One of the most interesting studies of the effect of athletic participation on student-athletes was conducted by sociologists Peter and Patricia Adler. The Adlers virtually became a part of a Division I basketball program for a five-year period. Their observations are outlined in their 1991 book entitled *Backboards and Blackboards: College Athletes and Role Engulfment*. Their conclusions were based upon extensive interviews and observation, and among those conclusions was the finding that after a four- or five-year intercollegiate athletic experience, student-athletes often had a much narrower "world view" than when they entered the university.

The Adlers found that upon initial enrollment, student-athletes had a broad range of interests and goals in the academic, social, and athletic areas. However, during their time on campus, they were forced to make decisions that pitted their academic and social interests against their athletic interests. Invariably, decisions were made in favor of athletic interests. For example, if a student-athlete wanted to go to a movie with a nonathlete, but the coach had planned a social event with someone who supported the athletic program, the student-athlete felt pressure to attend the team function. Or, if a coach thought a particular academic major was too demanding and would thus affect athletic performance, he would "suggest" that the student-athlete enroll in a less demanding major. Because of the intense and constant pressure to show one's "commitment to the program," student-athletes were continually forced to make decisions that would further their athletic goals, while pushing their academic and social aspirations into the background. Like the muscle that atrophies from inactivity, the result was a dwindling of student-athletes' social and academic interests in favor of athletic interests. Although certain activities, such as travel to new and exciting places, expand the student-athlete's "world view," the Adlers argued that the overall experience in some cases was actually to narrow the student-athlete's perspective.

> Despite its structural fit within the trends current in American society, the engulfment of college athletes raises questions and conflicts that cannot be easily answered. On the one hand, these young men are spending formative years sacrificing themselves to entertain and enrich others, lured by the hope of a future that is elusive at best. For other students, this kind of narrowing and intense focus may lead to a prosperous career in such fields as medicine, law, education, or business. For college athletes, however, their specialization, dedication, and abandonment of alternatives leads to their becoming finally proficient at a role that, for most, will end immediately following the

conclusion of their college eligibility. For those fortunate enough to achieve a professional career, the end comes only slightly later.

It is ironic that these athletes are partly socialized to failure; although some sustained the athletic role temporarily, they were released by the system at the end of four years engulfed in a role destined to become an "ex" (Ebaugh 1988). College athletes entered the university thinking that they would expand their horizons and opportunities in a variety of ways. They ended up narrowing their selves enough that their more grandiose expectations were not met. (Adler and Adler 1991, 230)

One of the purposes of college is to broaden the scope of young people's vision and to provide youth with opportunities to make decisions for themselves and hopefully to learn from even those decisions that turned out to be mistakes. College should expand horizons and teach young people the love of learning. Is it possible that involvement in highly competitive athletics might actually do the opposite? Does participation in intercollegiate athletics actually narrow focus and self-identity of young people, and restrict decision-making opportunities?

The preliminary results of a study led by Hans Steiner, a professor of psychiatry and behavioral science at Stanford University, shed some interesting light on the issue of "focus" in athletics. The study, released in 1996, is based on a survey of more than 2,100 high school and college students. It found that high school student-athletes earned better marks on a variety of psychological tests than did their peers who were not student-athletes. But a different picture emerged of the college student-athlete. The same psychological traits that could contribute to the success of college student-athletes on the playing fields and courts also put them at increased risk of drug or alcohol abuse, or academic and personal problems. According to Steiner, student-athletes are taught to repress the notion of failure, which does not contribute to good psychological health. Steiner plans to test his conclusions further with additional student-athletes and students.

The lengths to which coaches and administrators will go to keep their student-athletes focused on their sport can at times be amusing. During my junior year at Davidson, our basketball coach took a sudden and unexpected leave of absence. We returned from our short Christmas break to find that our coach was no longer going to be with us. Worse, none of the other coaches or administrators knew where he was, or if they did, they were not telling. After practice, an administrator addressed the team as follows: "Men, your coach is gone. Don't know where he is. Thinks he's got a brain infection. Thinks he's gonna die. . . . But I tell ya what we're gonna do. We're gonna buy you a big 'ole steak and we're gonna go out and beat Marshall."

Our coach, for whom we all cared deeply, was missing and apparently very sick. Yet foremost on the mind of this administrator was not helping us deal with, or even understand, what had happened to him. Rather the push was to get us focused on beating Marshall. Of course, feeding us a "big 'ole steak" was supposed to help us forget that our coach was missing and to ignore the fact that no one seemed to know where he was. We lost to Marshall by 30 points.

TEACHING HONESTY AND SPORTSMANSHIP

The promise of a fair and honest contest forms the foundation upon which athletic competition is allegedly based. Athletic participation, it is argued, naturally enhances a participant's moral and ethical development through the teaching of good sportsmanship. But research supporting this assertion has, to this point, been largely inconclusive. On the contrary, recent studies seem to suggest that the moral and ethical reasoning skills of intercollegiate athletes might actually be less developed than those of nonathletes.

Over the past few years, Jennifer Beller and Sharon Stoll, both of the University of Idaho's Center for Ethics, have evaluated thousands of high school and college student-athletes and their nonathlete peers on their cognitive moral reasoning development. Beller and Stoll have found that "revenue producing athletes, whether at NAIA, Division III, Division II or Division I are significantly lower in moral development than their peer group, and individual and non-revenue producing athletes." Further, they found that "revenue producing athletes are not morally, developmentally dysfunctional when they come to athletics, rather the competitive process appears to cause a masking of moral reasoning processes" (Stoll 1996).

The classic example of the "masking" of the moral reasoning process is pointed out by Stephen Carter in his 1996 book *Integrity*. During a televised football game, a player who had failed to catch a ball thrown his way hit the ground, rolled over, and then jumped up, celebrating as if he had made the catch. Screened from the play, the referee awarded the catch. A review of the replay revealed that the player had dropped the ball. The broadcaster commented, " What a heads up play!," meaning, in Carter's words, "Wow! What a great liar this kid is. Well done!"

> By jumping up and celebrating, he was trying to convey a false impression. He was trying to convince the officials that he had caught the ball. . . . So, in any understanding of the word, he lied. . . . Now, suppose the player had instead gone to the referee and said, "I'm sorry sir, but I did not make that catch. Your call is wrong." Probably his coach and teammates and most of his team's fans would have been furious: he

would not have been a good team player. The good team player lies to
the referee, and does so in a manner that is at once blatant (because
millions of viewers see it) and virtually impossible for the referee to
detect. Having pulled off this trickery, the player is congratulated: he is
told that he has made a heads-up play. Thus, the ethic of the game
turns out to be an ethic that rewards cheating. (Carter 1996, 5)

David L. Shields and Brenda J. Bredemeir from the University of California, Berkeley, reviewed the body of research available regarding sport and
character development in their book *Character Development and Physical
Activity*. Consider the following excerpt, which calls into question the blind
acceptance of the claim that athletics builds character.

Let us state our conclusion first. The research does not support either
position in the debate over sport building character. If any conclusion
is justified, it is that the question that is posed is too simplistic. The
term *character* is vague, even if modified with the adjective *good*. More
important, sport experience is far from uniform. There is certainly
nothing intrinsically character-building about batting a ball, jumping
over hurdles, or rolling heavy spheres toward pins. The component
physical behaviors of sport are not in themselves moral or immoral.
When we talk about building character through sport, we are referring
to the potential influence of the social interactions that are fostered by
the sport experience. The nature of those interactions varies from
sport to sport, from team to team, from one geographical region to
another, from one level of competition to another, and so on. . . . The
word *character* is often used synonymously with *personality*. Not surpris-
ingly, then, a number of early researchers were interested in whether
sport influenced the personality characteristics of participants. Most
studies conducted on this question have followed one or more of three
strategies (Stevenson 1975): a comparison of athletes with non-par-
ticipants, a comparison of elite athletes with less-advanced sport participants or the general population, or a comparison of athletes participating in different sports. In all three cases, results are inconclusive.
(Shields and Bredemeir 1995, 178)

Bredemeir and Shields went beyond assessing whether sport positively
affects the "character" of participants; they reviewed the research that
attempts to gauge sports participation on more narrowly defined traits such
as aggression, sportsmanship, compassion, fairness, and integrity. Once
again, they determined that in virtually all categories, the existing research
is inconclusive.

A notable exception, however, is research indicating a negative correlation between sport involvement and delinquency; the reason for the
correlation was unclear. Delinquency theory suggests that deviant behavior is learned through contact with other deviants. Thus, this correlation

might be inferred by the fact that sport participation deters delinquency by encouraging less frequent, shorter, or less intense interaction with deviant others. Even this apparent positive by-product of sport participation may not result from what is being taught on the playing fields but rather from the fact that the individual simply has less contact with "bad influences." That being the case, athletic participation would be no more likely to result in preventing deviant behavior than participation in other extracurricular activities such as band, theater, or the debate club.

If there is one general conclusion to be made from Bredemeir and Shields' work, it is that "whatever advantages or liabilities are associated with sport involvement, they do not come from sport per se, but from the particular blend of social interactions and physical activities that comprise the totality of the sport experience" (Shields and Bredemeir 1995, 184).

ATHLETIC INJURIES TO THE MIND

Present-day researchers are not the only ones who have questioned the "sports build character" myth. Brutus Hamilton, track and field coach at the University of California, Berkeley, from 1933 to 1965, was one of the all-time best coaches. Hamilton was also U.S. Olympic decathlon coach in 1932 and 1936 and head U.S. track and field coach for the 1952 Olympic games in Helsinki. Hamilton, known as a coach who kept life and athletics in perspective, worried more about character development than about winning. He expressed his concern regarding sports participation and its effect on an individual's character development in a unique way at a Marin Sports Injury Conference in 1962.

> Further athletic injuries to the boy's character can result in college. If he has chosen a school where sports are emphasized out of proportion to their importance he will find life easy if he performs well on the team. He will be coddled, made over, given parties by avid alumni, and even handed under-the-table payment, if not in cash then in some kind of presents. He's embarrassed at first, but soon comes to accept these things as a matter of course. The moral fiber gradually weakens and by the time his intercollegiate competition is over he is a victim of the system, a slave to gross and violent tastes, standing at the cross-roads of Destiny. He was yesterday's headlines; he will be tomorrow's trivia. Now comes the harsh test as he faces the cruel pace of this competitive world in what he considers routine, humdrum chores of business. He has no headlines now; others who are younger are taking his place. Some former athletes make the adjustment rather quickly, others grope for several years and then make the adjustment, usually with the help of some good woman. Others, all too many, drift into middle age and resort to artificial stimulation to substitute for the

intoxicating experiences they enjoyed in sports. Maybe sports were only partly to blame, but I believe no one would criticize a doctor who diagnosed these cases as an athletic injury to character suffered in youth. . . .

The sad cases though are the ones which involve the eager, bright lad who goes to college on some kind of an athletic grant and is eager to become an Engineer, Lawyer, Doctor, Teacher or Architect. He becomes a victim of the intensity of the athletic training program. He misses practice to work on problem sets or to write out a book report. The coach suggests that he may be in the wrong course. Maybe he should transfer to a course which is not so demanding on his time. He certainly can't miss any more practices or his grant may be terminated. The boy has little choice, so he submits to the coach's suggestion and gives up his planned career. He may succeed gloriously in this new field but always he will wonder if he didn't make a mistake. He will always consider that he suffered an athletic injury to his mind in college whether anyone else does or not. When the training for an intercollegiate team becomes so time consuming, so intense and so exhausting that it is no longer possible for the student in the sciences or professions to participate, then something is wrong. Someone, perhaps a great many, are suffering an athletic injury to the mind. (Walton 1992, 118-20)

Los Angeles Lakers forward Elden Campbell made a related point, but much more precisely. When asked if he had earned his degree from Clemson University, he supposedly responded, "No, but they gave me one anyway."

RACE AND VIOLENCE

The college athletic community has also used as an educational justification the fact that a tremendous number of minority, particularly black, youngsters have benefited from the educational opportunity afforded them through athletic scholarships. Coaches often argue that athletics is the most discrimination-free enterprise in our country, insisting that the only criteria relevant in their evaluation of a student-athlete's worth is his or her performance on the field or court. The relatively large percentage of black student-athletes, particularly in the sports of football and basketball, provides some credence to the claim that athletic programs are in fact meeting this justification. According to the 1996 NCAA Division I Graduation Rate Report, 44 percent of football, 60 percent of men's basketball, and 34 percent of women's basketball student-athletes are black (National Collegiate Athletic Association 1996, 622). While these numbers are impressive, trumpeting athletics' tolerance of diversity as a significant justification for its place on campus is suspect at best, particularly given the small percentage of minorities in coaching and administrative positions, and athletics' poor record on issues relating to gender equity. This issue is discussed more thoroughly in Chapter 5.

Finally, there is growing concern regarding the effect of athletic participation on the participant's ability to resolve off-the-field conflicts peacefully, with particular attention being paid to violence against women. Accounts of student-athletes physically abusing women appear in our nation's newspapers far too often. One of the few studies of student-athlete violence against women was published in May 1995 in *The Journal of Sport and Social Issues*. The article reviewed 107 cases of sexual assault reported at 30 NCAA Division I institutions from 1991 to 1993. At 10 schools, male student-athletes were accused in 19 percent of the assaults, although they comprised only 3.3 percent of the male student body (Crosset, Benedict, and McDonald 1995, 126-140). Although broad conclusions should not be drawn from such limited research, the study does raise a question. Could it be that student-athletes, conditioned to resolve on-the-field conflicts with violence, have a more difficult time resolving off-the-field conflicts peacefully?

THE ISSUE IS ENVIRONMENT

So what does all this mean for athletics' place within higher education? On one hand, there is the widely accepted notion that sports build character. Participation in college athletics, it is argued, teaches young people important lessons about teamwork, discipline, communication, and loyalty—all skills necessary for success beyond the playing field. For the most part, the public has bought fully into the concept. The supposed character-building benefits of sports have become a part of American folklore. From the mythical Frank Merriwell of Yale to the legendary Bud Wilkinson of Oklahoma, sports and those who play them embody the characteristics that make Americans "number one." Those who coach are sage mentors and molders of our future leaders. Those who play are inspirational heroes and role models.

On the other hand, many argue that college athletics is not about education, in the sense of character development, at all; sport is about money, power, ego, and doing whatever it takes to win. As Oglive and Tutko (1985) pointed out, sport is not educational simply because it is sport. Rather it is the environment within which sports participation occurs that influences the educational, moral, and ethical development of participants. Sport that is overemphasized in relation to other fields of endeavor, particularly when it is conducted under the banner of an educational institution, is harmful. Sport kept in the proper perspective, where the process of participation (education) is not subjugated by the game's result (winning), can be extremely positive.

Along with the notion of athletics as a character builder goes the belief that coaches are effective teachers and positive educational role models. There are, however, too many examples of coaches who force their student-athletes into less demanding majors or discourage them from fully investing in their educational experience. These coaches are more interested in winning next week's game than preparing their student-athletes for life after athletics. Far too many student-athletes discontinue their participation in college athletics after becoming disillusioned with "the system." These dropouts are dismissed as "not having what it takes to be a winner." The successes are a product of the system; the failures are the result of the individual's shortcomings. Coaches refuse to admit the fact that often the individual succeeds despite the system or that it can be the system, rather than the individual, that fails. Therefore, along with questioning sports as inherently character building, we must also accept the fact that a whistle around the neck does not serve to qualify a coach as an educator.

For close to 100 years, we have claimed that big-time athletics is linked to the educational mission of the university, that participation is educational for the student-athlete, and that coaches and athletic administrators are educators. That assumption, however, can no longer be accepted without question. The purpose in highlighting the rather inconclusive research regarding sports participation's effect upon personality development is, once again, not to attack athletics or to minimize its potential to influence young people positively, but rather to caution the athletic community regarding its cavalier use of the "sports build character" justification. If education is a primary justification for athletics being on the college campus, then the question we must concern ourselves with is whether the environment in our programs is conducive to the positive educational and personal development of the student-athlete. It is time for the college athletic community to seriously rethink how this component of its mission is approached and realized.

DOES ATHLETICS MAKE MONEY?

Concern regarding making ends meet financially has been as much a part of the history of American higher education as the classroom lecture. As noted earlier, the never-ending search for new revenue streams was the driving force behind athletics' acceptance into the higher education community.

With the introduction of athletics to the already economically hard-pressed colleges and universities of late 19th and 20th century America, the doctrine of good works [that revenues generated by intercollegiate athletics are so much greater than the cost of the sport that the entire college benefits financially] offered some hope of relief from further financial hardships. Along with claims concerning the educational value of athletics—that sport participation builds character and that it helps student grades—the financial rationale for sport programs eased the entry onto campus of athleticism, a program previously foreign to the cognitively oriented college and university of the era. (Chu, Segrave, and Becker 1985, 289)

A widely held belief is that major college athletic programs generate a huge surplus of revenue for universities through gate receipts, television revenue, and alumni contributions. Even at universities where programs operate at a deficit, the exposure generated through television and the media is thought to increase the institution's stature and generate public interest in the university. Such visibility, it is said, results in increased applications and curries favor with legislators and the surrounding community. The facts, however, paint a different picture.

When institutional support (salaries, cash, tuition waivers, etc.) is not included on the revenue side of the financial ledger, most Division I college athletic programs lose money. According to an NCAA-sponsored report, only 28 percent of Division I programs generate more revenues than they expend. Further, only 46 percent of the 89 Division I-A schools reporting generated a profit. (The total number of Division I-A programs, those with "big-time" football, is 108; Division I-AA has 119 members and I-AAA has 78.) Without general institutional support, barely more than one in four Division I athletic programs would be solvent. A more detailed accounting of the financial statistics from this report follows (Fulks 1995, 19, 33, and 47):

	Profit	Deficit	Even
Division I-A (n=89)	46%	52%	2%
Division I-AA (n=72)	13%	85%	2%
Division I-AAA (n=45)	18%	82%	0%

And, as institutions begin to appropriate the long-overdue resources necessary to meet the demands of Title IX and gender equity, future financial figures may become more sobering.

There is more to the issue of athletics as a sound institutional business investment. The National Association of College and University Business Officers (NACUBO) conducted an analysis of college athletics' finances in its 1993 report entitled *The Financial Management of Intercollegiate Athletics Programs.* The analysis brought to light additional concerns regarding university accounting procedures as they apply to athletic operations. The report concluded that current costs, as high as they are, may not yet be telling the entire financial story. Specifically, the report questioned the practice of institutions paying many indirect or overhead costs generated by the athletic department.

The report identified six data elements that represent indirect expenditures.

- Amortization of facilities (if owned by the university)
- Student support services (academic and financial assistance) provided by the institution
- Student health services provided by the institution
- Athletic staff salaries and benefits for staff employed in other departments
- Proportion of buildings and grounds maintenance
- Proportion of capital equipment used

The report went on to state that

> Interviews with personnel in 18 institutions across all athletics divisions showed that only one of these data elements, amortization of facilities, could be calculated with any degree of accuracy, and even then this could be done only by the four Division I-A institutions in the study. Given this difficulty, it seems likely that many indirect or "overhead" expenses attributable to athletics activities are borne by the university as a whole. In institutions that require other programs or divisions to bear their share of indirect costs, allowing athletics to escape this burden creates a basic inequity. (National Association of College and University Business Officers 1993, 20)

We can easily conclude that were athletics' accounting held to a common business standard where all direct and indirect expenses are charged against revenues, significantly fewer than the 28 percent of all Division I institutions would report an athletic department profit.

Inasmuch as athletics was formally and primarily incorporated into higher education for financial and business reasons, it is ironic that more often than not this "business proposition" is a bad one. A successful business generates more money than it expends. After looking at the numbers, the argument can be made that except for the elite programs, athletics actually drains financial resources from the university.

> A review of the reports published over the past decade indicates that, as a whole, American intercollegiate athletics programs are unable to support themselves and that most programs run a deficit. This finding

is not surprising in colleges that designate varsity sports as part of the educational budget and make no claim to seek massive crowds. It does warrant concern, however, when one looks at institutions that have established varsity football and/or basketball as major, self-supporting activities intended to produce revenues, with large arenas and stadia and with television audiences. (Thelin and Wiseman 1989, 15)

Due largely to reports of huge television deals and corporate sponsorship agreements, it is easy to assume that major college athletic programs are rolling in money. But based upon actual figures, the claim that athletic programs make money for the university is largely untrue. Yes, athletic programs generate revenue. And yes, occasionally we read about an athletic department writing a check to the university's library or general scholarship fund. But what is not as readily reported is that major college athletic programs also spend a tremendous amount of money, particularly in the sports of football and basketball.

Further, no conclusive evidence exists to prove that a successful athletic program results in increased alumni giving or applications. Yet, the athletic community continues to use the claim as a primary justification for its own existence. While a successful athletic program can be a factor in alumni giving and student applications, it is unlikely that it is as much of a factor as claimed by those in the athletic community. While an institution may experience an immediate, short-term jump in applications or financial support (more than likely earmarked specifically for the athletic program) after a particularly successful football or basketball season, the fact remains that most institutions will continue to attract quality students who, when they graduate, will donate money to their alma maters, with little regard to the quality or even existence of a big-time athletic program.

DOES ATHLETICS GENERATE POSITIVE VISIBILITY?

Despite the probability that collegiate athletics does not generate monies for the university in general, athletic programs do provide significant regional and national visibility and exposure for the university. Games are broadcast on radio and television to a national audience, and newspaper coverage is often extensive. "By 1900, the relationship between football and public relations had been firmly established and almost everywhere acknowledged as one of sport's major justifications" (Rudolph 1990, 385). Clearly, athletic programs generate significant public exposure for universities. What is not so clear, however, is whether that exposure contributes positively to public relations.

The truth has been well documented: all exposure generated through major college athletics is not positive. A striking example of this dichotomy occurred at Florida State University. In winning a national football championship by defeating the University of Nebraska in the 1994 Orange Bowl, FSU garnered a tremendous amount of positive publicity. A national championship in football was evidence of the university's commitment to excellence. FSU was the best in the nation. There was no reason to expect other programs offered by the university were of lesser quality.

But how quickly things can change. Shortly after the Orange Bowl victory, allegations that student-athletes were provided clothes and cash by agents while coaches "looked the other way" quickly changed the type of exposure the football program was generating. If winning a national football championship meant that Florida State University was a winner, what did allegations that the football program won the national championship while breaking NCAA rules mean?

Questions regarding the supposed positive effect of athletic department visibility on the university go beyond the bad publicity associated with a scandal. As will be discussed in detail in Chapter 7, the argument can be made that the exposure generated through athletics has little to do with advancing positive educational or institutional messages, but that instead such visibility is used simply to promote the specific goals of the athletic department.

Again, the purpose here is not to criticize unduly or to dismiss the positive impact an athletic program can have on a university, financially or otherwise. A well-run program can contribute to the mission of a university in ways that might not show up in the institutional balance sheet. Visibility and stature within the state legislature may in many cases have a positive impact on institutional efforts to attract state funding. And despite inconclusive evidence, a successful athletic team and the visibility it brings has the potential to attract students to campus on an occasional basis. In fact, as suggested in Chapter 1, such contributions must be given greater consideration when evaluating an institution's return on investment in athletics.

Given the financial statements and the inconclusive research regarding alumni giving and applications, however, coaches and athletic administrators can no longer assert without question that athletics is a positive financial proposition for the institution. That being the case, they must be prepared to address this financial reality as they are challenged to justify athletics' place on campus. Like golfing partners who, when playing for money, make each other putt those short distances that are "gimmes" when playing for fun, college athletics no longer has the benefit of the "financial gimme."

NOW THAT'S ENTERTAINMENT

For millions of people, intercollegiate athletic contests provide enjoyable, exciting entertainment. Whether attending a women's tennis match or watching the Final Four on television, the pageantry and spectacle of college athletics offers an exciting reprieve from the ordinary. If there is one thing about college athletics that almost everyone—critics and proponents, fans and faculty—can agree upon, it is that college sports is good entertainment.

College sports is also Big Entertainment. Simply consider the NCAA's current seven-year, $1.7 billion contract with CBS for the television rights to the NCAA Division I Basketball Tournament as proof that college sports is an entertainment Goliath. If that is not proof enough, stand outside any Southeastern Conference or Big Ten football stadium on a Saturday afternoon in the fall and feel the excitement of 80,000 fans preparing for a big game. Concession stands, T-shirt sales, program sales, tailgating, and ticket scalpers—all turning a buck on college athletics. Merchandising, television ratings, corporate sponsors, shoe contracts, media coverage, crowds cheering . . . now that's entertainment!

Entertaining students, alumni, and the surrounding community is indeed a valuable service that higher education provides the public; it should not be trivialized. Higher education's purpose is to serve the needs of society, and athletics' unqualified success in providing this service should be celebrated.

As university enrollments have increased and diversified, athletic teams have promoted institutional unity and "the old college spirit." The entire university family, from faculty, students, and local fans, to alumni living in faraway places, can usually rally around "Ole State" U's football team. And while the firing of a controversial coach or an NCAA investigation can splinter a campus, athletics usually serves a unifying function for the university community. At what other function does so much of the university community gather to rally around the institution? As Paul "Bear" Bryant, the legendary University of Alabama football coach, allegedly said, "Fifty thousand people don't come to watch English class."

> At games, students and other members of the community come together for a common purpose. They are united, at least for the duration of the contest. Personal differences, politics, even business matters may be put aside. Those gathered view themselves as the community, united against another community. Everyone pulls together, and in so doing, the community generates uncommon energy and commitment. With community members acting in unison with the force of passion,

for the very dignity of the community is at stake, the whole is more
than the sum of its parts. (Miracle and Rees 1994, 160)

There are, however, risks in relying on athletic teams to unify the campus
community. Institutions that use athletics to solve the problems of a
fragmented community run the risk of making athletics, and not academic
excellence, the primary purpose of the institution. Although a football or
basketball program can unite a university community in a way that an
English department cannot, the primary purpose of the institution remains
educational. In short, a winning football team does not make a quality
educational institution.

Further, placing such a heavy emphasis on the unifying function of
sports promotes a community mind-set that college athletics is more about
the fans and campus community than it is about the participation of
student-athletes. A successful team in terms of a won-loss record, although
pleasing to fans, alumni, and the media, may cover up fundamental problems within an athletic program, such as low graduation rates, illegal
activities, or abusive coaches. While a few wins may unite the campus
community in the short term, it may result in long-term disintegration of
community trust if the athletic department is not meeting its fundamental
educational responsibilities to its student-athletes or if it contradicts broader
institutional goals.

Thus, the question remains: Are the entertainment and unifying functions of athletics enough to justify athletics' prominence in the university
educational system?

WHAT DOES ALL THIS MEAN?

So where does this analysis of principles, missions, and justifications leave
us? After having reviewed athletics' three primary justifications for being a
part of the higher education community, the answer is still mixed. Whether
athletic departments are meeting their fundamental educational and per-
sonal-development responsibilities to student-athletes is questionable. Certainly, many coaches and athletic administrators are committed and effective teachers as well as positive educational role models. And thousands of
student-athletes earn a quality, well-balanced academic and athletic experience. But unfortunately, as a result of the "win-at-all-cost" mentality that
drives the athletic culture, some lessons learned through athletic participation are not positive. Thus, the assertion that participation in college
athletics is a positive educational experience can no longer be accepted
without question.

Regarding the claim that athletics generates money and visibility for the
university, the data are again mixed. While athletic programs generate

revenue, most do not generate more than they expend. And finally, not all the visibility that an athletic program brings to the university is positive. Just ask any president of a school that has been placed on NCAA probation.

Thus, only one of the justifications for athletics being a part of higher education is being fully met—the justification of providing entertainment. And ironically, even when using the current standard of measuring the success of an athletic program—championships won—the vast majority of universities fail miserably. The very nature of sport dictates that for every winner there is a loser. Only one team in every league hangs up the championship banner at season's end.

If our athletic programs are not successful in meeting their primary reasons for existence within higher education, we must reconsider how they can justify their existence. Moreover, because so few of our athletic programs achieve success as it is currently defined, we should reconsider whether the current standards of success—championship banners won and revenue generated—are reasonable and relevant. In short, we must go back to the drawing board and consider in fundamental terms just what our athletic programs should be about, what the people associated with these programs should represent, where these programs fit overall within higher education, and, most important, how their success should be measured.

References

Adler, Patricia A., and Peter Adler. 1991. *Backboards and Blackboards: College Athletes and Role Engulfment.* New York: Columbia University Press.

Carter, Stephen L. 1996. *Integrity.* New York: Basic Books.

Chu, Donald. 1989. *The Character of American Higher Education and Intercollegiate Sport.* Albany, NY: State University of New York Press.

Chu, Donald, Jeffrey Segrave, and Beverly Becker. 1985. *Sport and Higher Education.* Champaign, IL: Human Kinetics Publishers.

Crosset, Todd W., Jeffrey R. Benedict, and Mark A. McDonald. 1995. "Male Student-Athletes Reported for Sexual Assault: A Survey of Campus Police Departments and Judicial Affairs." *Journal of Sport and Social Issues* 19 (2).

Ebaugh, Helen R. 1988. *Becoming an Ex.* Chicago. University of Chicago Press.

Fulks, Daniel L. 1995. *Revenues and Expenses of Intercollegiate Athletic Programs: Financial Trends and Relationships.* Overland Park, KS: NCAA.

Miracle, Andrew, and C. Roger Rees. 1994. *Lessons of the Locker Room: The Myth of School Sports.* Amherst, NY: Prometheus Books.

National Association of College and University Business Officers. 1993. *The Financial Management of Intercollegiate Athletics Program.* Washington, DC: NACUBO.

National Collegiate Athletic Association. 1996. *1996 NCAA Division I Graduation-Rates Report.* Overland Park, KS: NCAA.

Oglive, Bruce, and Thomas Tutko. 1985. "Sport: If You Want to Build Character, Try Something Else." In *Sport and Higher Education,* edited by Donald Chu, Jeffrey Segrave, and Beverly Becker. Champaign, IL: Human Kinetics Publishers.

Rudolph, Frederick. 1990. *The American College and University: A History*. Athens, GA: University of Georgia Press.

Savage, Howard J., et al. 1929. *American College Athletics*. New York: Carnegie Foundation.

Shields, David L., and Brenda J. Bredemeir. 1995. *Character Development and Physical Activity*. Champaign, IL: Human Kinetics Publishers.

Steiner, Hans. 1991. Research results reported in *The Stanford Daily*, May 7 1996.

Stevenson, C.L. 1975. Socialization Effects of Participation in Sports: A Critical Review of the Research. *Research Quarterly*, 46, 287–301.

Stoll, Sharon. Letter to John Gerdy. 19 July 1996.

Thelin, John R., and Lawrence L. Wiseman. 1989. *The Old College Try: Balancing Athletics and Academics in Higher Education*. Report No. 4. Washington, DC: The George Washington University.

Walton, Gary M. 1992. *Beyond Winning: The Timeless Wisdom of Great Philosopher Coaches*. Champaign, IL: Leisure Press.

PART TWO

· · · · · · · · · · ·

The Principles of the New Standard

CHAPTER

Rethinking Student-Athlete Welfare

Don't give me all of that stuff about character building, about opportunity for education. Only a small percentage of athletes in many of our football and basketball programs are graduating! Sure—athletics help bring the campus community together, that sort of thing; but the only thing that validates their presence is the learning experiences the student receives. And if that's not happening, we've just failed, and we lack credibility with the public.

President of an NCAA Division I Institution
(Bailey and Littleton 1991, 32)

A s related in Chapter 4, skepticism regarding the supposed educational benefits of participation in highly competitive athletics remains high. With the ever increasing pressure on coaches and athletic administrators to win and generate money, the interests of the very people college athletics allegedly benefits most—student-athletes—no longer seem to be of primary importance. As a result, the implicit agreement struck between the student-athlete and the institution—athletic performance for a legitimate opportunity to earn a meaningful degree and well-rounded college experience—may be out of balance, and if so, the student-athlete is receiving the short end of the deal.

The implications for this short shrifting of the student-athlete are far-reaching, not only in terms of the way the public views the situation, but more important, because of the effect it has on the athletic community's ability to develop and maintain credibility within higher education. Inasmuch as the commitment to teaching—to developing our country's human resource—is the fundamental principle upon which education is based, to be found lacking in so basic an area of responsibility is particularly damning. Therefore, athletic departments must reconsider their educational commitment and responsibility to their student-athletes. The first principle necessary in implementing the New Standard is to return the student-athlete's educational welfare to its rightful place—at the center of our athletic programs. In short, our programs must be "about the student-athlete."

THE STUDENT-ATHLETE/INSTITUTIONAL AGREEMENT

The promise of a quality education is at the core of the bargain struck with the student-athlete when he or she signs a National Letter of Intent. The student-athlete provides athletic performance so the university can fill stadiums, appear on television, and provide entertainment for alumni, fans, and friends. In exchange for those services, the university and its administrators and coaches provide the student-athlete a genuine opportunity to earn a meaningful degree and a well-balanced athletic, academic, and social experience.

Student-athletes have kept their end of the agreement. Stadiums are full, television cameras are focused on the action, and money is being generated. It is arguable, however, whether universities are meeting their end of the bargain. As outlined in Chapter 4, rather than providing a well-rounded educational experience designed to prepare student-athletes for success in the world-after-athletics, the college athletic experience might actually program student-athletes for failure.

The agreement between student-athlete and the institution is a fair one only if both sides meet their obligations. Unfortunately, a fundamental inconsistency in the relationship between the institution and student-athlete has to this point prevented the execution of a fair agreement. Compounding this problem is the refusal of the college athletic community even to acknowledge, let alone amend, this inconsistency. The fact is that, despite what we say, the interests of those responsible for operationalizing the agreement—coaches and athletic administrators on the one hand and student-athletes on the other—are, for the most part, diametrically opposed.

Coaches are hired to win games. If coaches do not win games, they are fired. Athletic administrators must help their coaches win games to fill stadiums and generate revenue to pay for the athletic program and to satisfy alumni demands for a winning program. If the athletic director does not meet the budget, he or she is soon out of a job. Thus, coaches and athletic directors' goals are short term and economically driven, centered upon next week's game.

What is in the best interest of the student-athlete, however, is to prepare for the next 50 years of life. As is always the case when balancing short- and long-term goals, conflicts arise. These conflicts have nothing to do with "the good guys" versus "the bad guys"; they are simply the structural realities of big-time college athletics. There is not a coach in the country who does not want every student-athlete under his or her tutelage to graduate and at the same time to win games. The problem, however, is that it all eventually comes back to winning games. It is easy to understand why coaches and athletic administrators are primarily interested in maximizing the student-athlete's athletic performance. For coaches and athletic administrators, athletics is a full-time job. For student-athletes, it is, or should be, a part-time job. The end result is that this intense pressure to win to generate the revenue necessary to support large athletic budgets pits the social and academic interests of student-athletes against the interests of the athletic department, especially in football and basketball.

> Typically, in Division I, these sports (football and basketball) are supposed to produce a surplus of income in order to support themselves and other sports in the athletic program (and sometimes even other programs in or associated with the university). As well, they are to enhance the public image of the university, producing a number of supposedly positive outcomes (increased applications, enhanced contributions, etc.). These missions are sometimes in conflict with the goal of providing an educational environment for the athlete. Frequently, those benefits that were historically incidental by-products become the principal goals, and the educational benefits to the athlete become lost in the process. (Kjeldsen 1992, 105)

Yes, we have created scholar-athlete awards to highlight academic achievement. Yes, NCAA schools are now required to report the graduation rates of their student-athletes. And yes, many schools have implemented the NCAA-sponsored "Life Skills" program, which is a student support system designed to focus on the individual as a whole: academically, athletically, and emotionally. This program represents the most comprehensive compilation of resources available to directors of student-athlete support programs and will no doubt contribute in a positive manner to student-athlete welfare. But there is far more to making athletic programs "about the student-athlete" than a few new programming ideas and scholar-athlete awards.

If the student-athlete/institutional agreement continues to be less than fair, even with these improvements, what else can athletic departments do to ensure that their programs are "about the student-athlete?"

To make the student-athlete/institutional agreement a fair one will require a fundamental shift in the way athletic departments approach issues of student-athlete welfare, not only programmatically or legislatively, but also philosophically. We must rethink at a fundamental level the way we perceive and treat student-athletes, our expectations of them, and the messages we send them. Offered in this chapter are not only specific programmatic and legislative initiatives but also some suggestions for fundamental philosophical changes in the way we approach student-athlete welfare. If incorporated into the athletic community's "mind-set," these changes will result in a more balanced student-athlete/institutional agreement.

WE MUST BE HONEST

If the student-athlete/institutional agreement is ever to be a fair one, we must be honest. Coaches and athletic directors are evaluated on short-term results: games won, money generated, and budgets balanced. We can no longer ignore the fact that a standard which mandates these results often does not allow the long-term best interests of student-athletes to be the primary purpose of athletic programs. We must stop lying to ourselves so that we can begin to be honest with our student-athletes about the inherent conflicts in the system.

Being honest with student-athletes about the harsh realities of the major college athletic experience will result in a greater likelihood that they will build relationships with individuals outside the athletic department. If student-athletes understand that coaches' advice, while well intentioned, is often clouded by self-interest, they will be more inclined to seek advice on nonathletic matters from faculty members and academic administrators who have no stake in the athletic department.

The two elements of the student-athlete experience are the academic/social and the athletic. The athletic department holds authority over the athletic component and in that role influences the student-athlete in ways that will maximize the individual's athletic performance and development. That is as it should be. But to have the athletic department also exert virtually complete control over the academic/social half of the student-athlete experience undermines the likelihood of the student-athlete achieving a well-balanced educational experience. When academic or social interests conflict with athletic concerns, student-athletes are made to understand that it is their athletic interests that are of primary importance, particularly since the athletic department is "paying the freight" with a scholarship. Although inexcusable, it is understandable for coaches to use their influence in this way because they are under pressure to win.

But does the fact that the athletic department funds the scholarship mean the athletic department owns the student-athlete? The bargain between the student-athlete and the institution is athletic performance for a legitimate chance to earn a meaningful degree and a well-balanced athletic and academic experience. To have such an experience, the student-athlete must develop a support system outside as well as inside the athletic department. If the student-athlete's college experience extends no further than the locker room doors, the likelihood of the student-athlete/institutional agreement being balanced is virtually nonexistent.

For example, when a student-athlete is faced with a decision that relates to an academic, social, or personal matter, he or she will most likely approach a coach for advice. Throughout their careers athletes have consistently been told that "coach knows best." And, most times, the coach gives sound counsel. But no matter how well intentioned the coach's advice may be, there is a strong possibility that it will be biased by some athletic motivation. Therefore, after hearing from the coach, the student-athlete must be encouraged to seek guidance from others, especially family members, faculty, and academic administrators. Encouraging student-athletes to develop a nonathletic support system allows them to obtain a viewpoint unclouded by athletic motivations or considerations. With other views as reference points, the student-athlete is equipped with the perspective necessary to make a more informed decision. We must allow student-athletes to make such decisions, and those decisions must be respected. It is part of "the bargain."

Encouraging student-athletes to build relationships outside the athletic department also makes good business sense. Most athletic departments are trying to limit the number of transfer student-athletes and increase their graduation rates. Research on student retention largely indicates that a major factor in students leaving an institution is the feeling of personal isolation. Given that a significant number of student-athletes, particularly in the sports of football and basketball, report "frequent" or "occasional" feelings of isolation (32.5 percent of those in housing with other student-athletes and 23.4 percent of those in housing with mostly other students) (National Collegiate Athleic Association 1988), athletic departments should intensify efforts to encourage student-athletes to build relationships outside the department.

Student-athletes must be told that although athletic departments have a responsibility to create an atmosphere that is conducive to academic achievement, the interests and motivations of coaches and athletic administrators are different from theirs. We often deny this reality, claiming that student-athletes are not interested in such truths because their only desire is to play professional ball. Such a claim is a myth. Most student-athletes want to earn a degree. According to the 1988 NCAA *Studies of Intercollegiate Athletes*, upon enrollment, 95 percent of football and basketball student-athletes and 93 percent of participants in other sports reported that obtaining a degree was of "importance" or "greatest importance" (National Collegiate Athletic Association 1988, 11).

Many will argue that such statistics are inflated and that student-athletes are simply saying the "right" thing. Once they arrive on campus, they will behave in ways that do not support their earlier claims. Such a skeptical viewpoint is an example of how we sell student-athletes short and how our attitudes ultimately contribute to such behavior. Rather than reacting with skepticism, we should celebrate the fact that student-athletes at least know and will say that academics are important to them. The more responsible reaction would be to encourage this positive notion with attitudes and actions that communicate to student-athletes that their first priority should be to earn a degree. With encouragement, they will be more likely to follow up such statements with responsible academic behavior. Our response should be one of encouragement, affirmation, and full support rather than a skepticism that suggests that they are either lying or incapable of having a genuine interest in getting more from their college experience than a few newspaper clippings and a fat pro contract. Yes, some only give lip service to the importance of obtaining a degree, but simply to dismiss this statistic and suggest that getting a degree is not of great importance to the majority of student-athletes is educationally irresponsible.

Being honest regarding the realities of major college athletics will be difficult because in being honest coaches will be forced to relinquish a degree of control over their student-athletes. Letting go of control is particularly difficult for a coach who sat in parents' livingrooms and promised to look after and "protect" their children. But if asked, most parents would prefer that those relating to their children be honest with them, for honesty is empowering.

If colleges do nothing more than inform student-athletes that their interests (getting a degree) are often at odds with the interests of coaches (winning) and athletic administrators (generating revenues), the value of their intercollegiate athletic experience from an educational and personal development standpoint will improve significantly. Being honest regarding this fundamental conflict of interests will better enable student-athletes to approach their college athletic experience with their eyes open.

RECRUITING

Honesty begins during the recruitment process. The lifeblood of a success-ful athletic program is recruiting. Coaches are under tremendous pressure to sign quality high-school student-athletes. Because most assistant coaches are hired and evaluated on their ability to "deliver" top-notch prospects, it is no wonder they will do or say most anything to convince a young person to sign on the dotted line. There are countless stories about the outrageous ends to which coaches will go to land a top recruit. For example, a coach will never mention anything negative about his or her institution because a rosy picture must be painted for the prospect, regardless of whether that picture represents reality.

"What are your graduation rates, coach?" a prospective student might ask.

"Good, really good," answers the coach.

"How about your academic support program?"

"The best in the country. We spare no expense."

"I am interested in majoring in engineering. How's your engineering program?"

"Excellent, one of the best in the country."

"Biology is a tough major, and I may need to take some lab classes that might interfere with practice time. Will I be able to do that?"

"Of course. We'll do whatever we must to get you that degree, I promise."

"What is the atmosphere for minorities on campus, coach?"

"Great. You'll really feel at home here."

"Are you going to be at this school for my four years?"

"Absolutely. I am totally committed to State U."

"Am I the only player you are recruiting for this position?"

"Yup, you are number one. Numero Uno!"

"Will I start as a freshman?"

"If you come to State, you will start, be an All American, and probably a first round draft choice for the pros."

"Yeah, right, coach."

Although one might expect coaches to stretch the truth regarding athletic matters, such as playing time, misrepresenting an academic pro-gram or the informal character of the social and intellectual communities that exist on a campus is an entirely different issue. According to Vincent Tinto, one of the foremost authorities on student retention, "It is precisely that informal world of student life that many times spells the difference between staying and leaving [the institution]" (Tinto 1993, 159). A mis-represented athletic situation might adversely affect a student-athlete for the four or five years he or she participates in college athletics. Misrepresenting an academic program or what student life will be like could adversely affect that same individual for life.

The foundation for successful adjustment to college, particularly for the student-athlete, is set during the recruitment process. In fact, Tinto identified a student's "first formal contact with the institution" as a major factor not only in whether a student chooses to attend a school but also whether that student remains at that school. "The formation of unrealistic or mistaken expectations . . . may lead to eventual departure by setting into motion a series of largely malintegrative interactions based upon the perception by the individual of either having been misled or having seriously erred in his/her choice of college" (Tinto 1993, 155). Being honest during the recruiting process is important not only because it is the right thing to do, but also because it greatly affects student retention. "Though the painting of a 'rosy picture' may, in the short run, increase enrollment, it is very likely, in the long run, to decrease retention by widening the gap between promise and delivery" (Tinto 1993, 155).

Not only should coaches be honest with prospects during recruitment, but institutions must insist that their coaches have a thorough understanding of the institution's academic programs and campus culture prior to allowing them to represent the institution as recruiters. Coaches must be cautioned not to bluff responses, but to say instead, "I'll get back to you," when they do not know the answers to questions about academic and student-life issues. Student-athlete prospects have the same right as all other student prospects to be informed accurately of the academic opportunities available at the institution.

In most cases, coaches do not knowingly misrepresent an academic program or what campus life will be like for the student-athlete. More often, coaches simply do not take an interest in, or are not informed about, an institution's major requirements, student service programs, or the unique cultural aspects of the institution. What information coaches relay and how they communicate with prospects is not something to be taken lightly. It is no surprise that a major cause of student-athlete discontent stems from a feeling that "the coach told me it would be different! He lied to me!" The adjustment from the highly recruited, pampered high-school senior to the lowly freshman often leads to feelings of disillusionment and a sense of having been misled by the coach during recruitment. Misrepresenting programs the university offers or shading the realities of the student-athlete experience at that institution can make what is a difficult adjustment to college for all students a particularly difficult adjustment for student-athletes.

ORIENTATION—MORE MISREPRESENTATION

The student-athlete's first semester or quarter on campus is critical in setting the stage for a productive, enjoyable college experience. Many students' study patterns, social habits, and attitudes regarding their school are formed during their initial weeks on campus. That being the case, an institutional commitment to providing an honest and thorough orientation experience is critical if our programs are to be "about the student-athlete." The central issue regarding the orientation of student-athletes relates to the common practice of athletic departments "managing," or worse yet actually "conducting," student-athlete orientation programs.

Many well-intentioned athletic departments develop orientation programs for student-athletes. However, such programs are not nearly as comprehensive as university-wide orientation programs. More significant, however, is the fact that when the athletic department administers the orientation program, it sets the unhealthy precedent that it will "take care of" everything for the student-athlete, including matters relating to academics and student life.

If student-athletes' long-term academic and social interests are being given full consideration, it is more beneficial for them to participate in a university-administered orientation program than one conducted by the athletic department. Orientation is not nearly as meaningful when the student-athlete is seated in a room full of freshmen teammates. Participating in a university-wide program provides a much more accurate picture of student life and the wide diversity of campus opportunities available to all students, including student-athletes.

Although the actual information that is disseminated as part of orientation programs is important, critical to the experience is the group with which the student-athlete participates in the program. Orientation represents an important opportunity to set a positive tone for future integration into the campus community, which, according to Tinto, is another key element in student retention.

> Here in the realm of interpersonal affiliation lies one of the keys to effective orientation programs, indeed to effective retention programs generally. Namely, that they go beyond the provision of information per se to the establishment of early contacts for new students not only with other members of their entering class but also with other students, faculty and staff of the institution. In this manner, effective orientation programs function to help new students make the often difficult transition to the world of the college and help lay the foundation for the development of the important personal linkages which are the

basis for the eventual incorporation of the individual into the social and intellectual life of the institution. (Tinto 1993, 159)

Student-athlete participation in university-administered orientation programs will raise the issue of missed practice time. Although coaches will insist that preseason practice is a crucial time to teach athletic fundamentals, it is far more important for the long-term personal and academic development of the student-athlete to learn the fundamentals of being a student on a college campus. Freshmen missing a few preseason practices will not cause an athletic program to crumble. Full and active participation in a university-run orientation program should be mandatory, as this is clearly an academic welfare issue and, as such, a situation in which the athletically driven motivations of coaches should take a back seat to the academic interests of the student-athlete.

BEYOND ORIENTATION—INFORMING THE STUDENT-ATHLETE

Mandating participation in institutional orientation programs and being honest during recruitment are critical first steps in creating a healthy academic and social environment for student-athletes. There is, however, much more to providing student-athletes the information necessary to achieve a quality, well-balanced college experience. Specifically, institutions must continue to inform student-athletes of the realities of the major college athletic experience throughout their college careers. This commitment to create an athletic department environment where student-athletes are encouraged to think critically regarding the various issues that are unique to their college experience will be what separates programs "about the student-athlete" from those not about them.

Being honest with student-athletes will present significant challenges for an athletic department, particularly its coaches. Will a more informed student-athlete ask more questions and challenge the status quo? Yes. Will an empowered student-athlete have more courage to question coaches and administrators and challenge athletic policy? Yes. But isn't that what our colleges and universities are supposed to be about? Yes. Isn't it the responsibility of educators to foster an environment for their students where critical thinking and healthy debate is encouraged? Yes!

Informing student-athletes regarding NCAA rules is only a starting point. Institutions must go beyond this to challenge student-athletes to think critically about their college athletic experience and the many issues related to being a highly visible student on a college campus. Student-athletes must be made to feel free to ask questions and to challenge preexisting assumptions, policies, and practices. Conducting forums, seminars, and classes to address issues such as ethics in recruiting, drug testing, and the changing coach/student-athlete relationship will empower student-athletes to be active participants in the intercollegiate athletic experience both intellectually and physically. Only when institutions commit themselves to creating an environment where dialogue and questions are welcome, critical thinking is encouraged, and personal responsibility is fostered will athletic programs fully realize their educational purpose.

What does it mean to be bought and paid for as a full scholarship student-athlete in a revenue-generating sport? Should student-athletes be paid? Is it cheating if you do not get caught? Why are student-athletes the only students on campus who are drug tested? Is the "win-at-all-cost" philosophy appropriate in the higher education setting? Do student-athletes have responsibilities as role models? Is the authoritarian management style appropriate on an athletic team or in a business setting? These are questions that can be used to challenge student-athletes to think critically about their place on a college campus. We should encourage student-athletes to contemplate critically and to discuss such issues in the hope that they will learn and grow from the dialogue. In short, the issues facing student-athletes offer some rich subject matter from which to teach.

How can student-athletes be challenged to think critically rather than simply obey? A start would be to use the signing of the NCAA student-athlete statement as a meaningful teaching opportunity. Rather than marching an entire football team in to review the rules and sign the form, all in an hour's time, smaller groups could be formed to discuss over an entire afternoon the principles and responsibilities outlined in the document. The common response to the student-athletes' questions regarding why they must sign the documents is, "Because if you don't, you can't play." End of lesson. How much more positive it would be to view the afternoon as an opportunity to teach.

Another way to challenge student-athletes to think is to conduct seminars addressing current issues in intercollegiate athletics. Student-athlete committees that are functional and legitimate rather than simply ceremonial could be operationalized. Classes that explore the types of issues mentioned above should be offered for credit. These need not be "crib" courses for jocks housed in the physical education department and taught by a coach; rather, they could be rigorous courses housed in the sociology, psychology, or education department under faculty control. The faculty control curriculum, and only they can assure that such courses are rigorous, meaningful, and deserving of academic credit.

A syllabus for such a course might cover the following topics:

- The Student-Athlete Ideal: Myth or Reality?
- Student-Athlete Rights
- The NCAA's Principles of Student-Athlete Welfare
- Medical Policies and the Right to Control Your Own Body
- To Pay or Not to Pay Student-Athletes
- Race in Sport
- Title IX and Gender Equity
- Why Drug Testing
- The Coach as Educator
- The "Business" of College Athletics
- Services and Activities Outside the Athletic Department
- Student-Athletes as Role Models
- Survival Strategies for the Student and the Athlete

Faculty cringe at the thought of awarding student-athletes credit for such courses, but if rigorous and under tight faculty control, courses like these can challenge student-athletes to think critically regarding their student-athlete experience. Only until they are challenged to approach the college athletic experience with their eyes open will student-athletes be able to place in context the lessons taught on the playing field relating to ethics, sportsmanship, and personal responsibility. Although many coaches would prefer student-athletes to obey their commands blindly, student-athletes must be encouraged to think for themselves and must not be afraid to ask, "Why?" Thought-provoking courses can be meaningful and worthy of course credit, and they would allow the student-athlete to be an active participant in the intercollegiate athletic experience, both physically and intellectually.

Those interested in keeping student-athletes uninformed will claim that such additional offerings are unnecessary, and that they only serve to further crowd the already full schedules of student-athletes. These critics argue that athletic departments offer more than enough seminars in time management and study skills. Moreover, they argue, student-athletes do not avail themselves of the opportunity to discuss these issues in informational meetings conducted by athletic departments, so why should they be expected to be interested in special courses and seminars on the same issues. While workshops in time management and study skills and briefings regarding NCAA rules are important, none of them truly challenge the student-athlete to think critically about the difficult issues that most affect their lives. If shortage of time is an issue, why not cancel or shorten some of the "voluntary" workouts, film sessions, or weight-training classes that are, in reality, "mandatory" activities?

In reality, something far more disturbing is going on here—something that cheats student-athletes both personally and intellectually. Specifically, it is an attitude that discourages the idea of special courses to teach student-athletes to think critically about their lives. If such courses and seminars are well structured, and if the institution commits to making these offerings interesting and meaningful, student-athletes can be expected to respond thoughtfully and enthusiastically. Student-athletes, like all other students, are interested in issues that affect their own lives. For educators to say that student-athletes lack such interest is irresponsible.

Sadly, coaches and athletic administrators are not interested in having their student-athletes discuss and question topics that cause them to become more informed about the realities of major college athletics. Creating a program environment where student-athletes are encouraged to evaluate their college experience critically is simply not in the coach's best interest. Or so he or she may think. A more informed student-athlete is a more independent student-athlete. A more introspective student-athlete is much less likely to accept without question what his or her coach relates as the gospel truth. Rather than seeking actively to engage student-athletes in critical analysis of such issues, coaches on the whole prefer not only to avoid such discussion of new possibilities, but discourage it at every level. Many coaches, unfortunately, are not particularly interested in developing a more enlightened student-athlete because such athletes make their jobs more difficult.

Encouraging student-athletes to think more independently while maintaining their respect for authority will undoubtedly make coaching and administering athletic programs more demanding. However, the prospect of being challenged by a more informed student-athlete should not threaten an educator. Educators not only disseminate information and promote the love of learning, they also have a strong desire to learn themselves. We educators must be willing to allow our student-athletes to challenge us because a more informed student-athlete can also teach. Only when we create an athletic department environment where information flows freely, critical thinking is encouraged, and an appreciation for the world outside athletics is fostered will the tremendous potential of athletics as a tool to educate be fully realized. Only until student-athletes are empowered to be full, active, and informed participants in their intercollegiate athletic experience, both on and off the playing fields, will the principle that college athletics is "about the student-athlete" become a reality.

TEACHING PERSONAL RESPONSIBILITY

In addition to being honest with student-athletes, we must also begin to teach personal responsibility in earnest. While the main focus of this discourse has been on the institution's role in academic matters, student-athletes also have personal responsibility for their own education. One example is their responsibility for attending class. Another is taking advantage of the various academic and personal development programs offered by the institution. Student-athletes must work hard academically. They must earn their education. In many cases, we have not insisted that they meet their responsibilities. We have preferred to "take care of them." Granted, there are risks in providing student-athletes the freedom to develop the decision-making skills necessary for responsible adulthood. But despite these risks, an increased effort on the parts of coaches, administrators, and students is necessary if the development of personal responsibility is to be realized as part of a quality, well-balanced education.

For example, in the "take care of them" mode, we often send another student or staff member to student-athletes' rooms to wake them up for class. We check their class attendance, and we give them countless second chances. But at some point, such babysitting works against instilling personal responsibility. While coaches are inclined to do everything possible to help a young person succeed, in the end, those who assume absolutely no personal responsibility for their own academic welfare must be allowed to fail. Even the "stars" must be permitted to fail. Such a lesson in personal responsibility will potentially result in "saving" other members of the team.

Coaches' reluctance to give up control and thereby risk failure is exacerbated by the expectation that others view them as responsible for the academic and social behavior of their student-athletes. If a student-athlete is arrested for shoplifting, the finger of blame is invariably pointed at the coach. Such an expectation of a coach places him or her in a tough position. Nevertheless, coaches must allow themselves to be challenged to walk the fine line between pushing the student-athlete out of the "athletic nest" by encouraging independent thought and responsibility, while maintaining the necessary discipline to elicit maximum athletic performance. If college athletics is to be about education, as has been claimed by athletic departments over and over, then coaches must begin to let student-athletes make decisions for themselves and be willing to live with the consequences.

Obviously, not all decisions made by college students are good ones. Nevertheless, it bears repeating that being held accountable for the decisions one makes, both good and bad, is a major part of the college experience. Fortunately, colleges offer a sheltered environment within which to make mistakes. In many cases, the penalties assessed within the college judicial system (e.g., suspension or academic probation) are significantly less stringent than penalties assessed in the "real world" where jail or the loss of a job are not uncommon consequences. As difficult as it may be to surrender control, it is absolutely essential that coaches and others in administration do so. While other students within the university community are making decisions about academics, living arrangements, whether to cut class, and when to go to bed at night, student-athletes more often are having virtually all decisions made for them by their athletic departments.

I personally got a sobering taste of the result of an athletic department taking care of everything for their student-athletes during a season of professional basketball with the Maine Lumberjacks of the Continental Basketball Association. Upon the completion of preseason training camp, I set out to secure more permanent living arrangements because the team was no longer willing to pay for and arrange our training camp lodging. I will never forget how bewildered a fellow teammate was when faced with the simple task of finding an apartment. He had no idea of how to go about renting an apartment, having a phone connected, or paying a deposit for utilities. This teammate was someone who had spent four years on a college campus! While many college graduates have never rented an apartment, most, when the time comes, take personal responsibility for finding out how to do so. My teammate, however, had become accustomed to having things arranged for him, and those things include living arrangements. Such an expectation is clearly not appropriate for success in the "real world."

In many cases, even the most fundamental decisions—their daily schedule; where, when, and what they eat; or when they go to bed and wake up—are made for student-athletes by coaches intent upon keeping their student-athletes' focus upon their athletic performance. The result is that student-athletes' sense of personal responsibility is stunted, and they proceed through their college athletic experience as active participants athletically, but passive participants intellectually. Again, the fundamental justification for athletics—that it is a tool to educate—is compromised.

THE MESSAGES WE SEND

Finally, all this means that we must reconsider the messages we send student-athletes. While we talk to student-athletes about the importance of education, we are sending, through our daily actions, an entirely different message. Take, for example, the physical environment within which student-athletes spend their days. The locker room, weight room, athletic offices, study halls, and meeting rooms are decorated with trophies commemorating athletic achievements, pictures of current and ex-athletes, a

"Wall of Fame" decorated with pictures of former student-athletes cur-rently in the pros—all daily reminders of athletic accomplishments. In one Division I-A athletic complex, a four-foot-high National Football League logo is displayed on the wall. At another football complex, a special meeting room is set aside just for NFL scouts to view film. The room is labeled the "NFL Room." One is hard-pressed to find a picture of a student-athlete in a cap and gown. We talk education, but our actions say nothing but athletics.

Consider, for example, the awards we give student-athletes—trophies, watches, and sweatsuits. I cannot recall the number of watches I received as awards while in college, but I do know that had I saved them, by the time I graduated I could have worn a different watch every day of the week. How many different sweatsuit outfits does a student-athlete need? Again, one for each day of the week seems to be the standard we shoot for. How about an award that supports excellence in education such as a leather bound, engraved dictionary, a thesaurus, or an atlas? Although a small and seem-ingly insignificant gesture, it delivers a different message.

And how about the things coaches say to student-athletes? "If you wanted an education you should have gone to Harvard." "You came to school to play football. You could have stayed home if you wanted an education." "I know it's finals week and you should be doing that academic stuff, but try to stay focused on basketball." "You're not smart enough to make it in college, so you're going to have to learn how to cheat."

The following incredible exchange actually took place between a stu-dent-athlete and a coach who was concerned that the student was missing too many "voluntary" summer workouts because of a class conflict.

> Assistant Coach: "You need to be at those workouts."
>
> Student-athlete: "I have a class."
>
> Assistant Coach: "You need to be at those workouts."
>
> Student-athlete: "You telling me to cut class?"
>
> Assistant Coach: "Well, do they check?"
>
> Student-athlete: "I thought academics came first?" (reference to a statement made to the team by the head coach)
>
> Assistant Coach: "You ever say that again, you can pack your bags."

All the above statements were direct quotes from coaches as related by student-athletes to various academic advisers at Division I-A programs.

The message can be particularly clear when a student-athlete must leave practice early to attend class. "Just 10 more minutes. One more set of drills," orders the coach. The student-athlete complies and is late for class.

The same coach, who would not accept a student-athlete being late for a team meeting, does not care that the student-athlete is late for class. The message is simple: Athletics is more important than academics.

Travel does not serve the student-athlete's academic interests either. Tournaments and championships frequently occur during exam periods. Basketball games are scheduled to begin at 9:30 p.m. on a week night to accommodate television programming. How many students are going to be ready to learn at 8:00 a.m. after returning to campus from a long road trip at 3:00 a.m.? How many are even going to be in class at 8:00 a.m. after such a trip? The message is simple. When push comes to shove, athletics takes precedence over academics.

Even something as seemingly simple as how coaches and athletic administrators refer to student-athletes as "players" or "athletes" rather than as "students" or "student-athletes" says volumes about how we view student-athletes. How can we expect the media, the faculty, the public, and most important, student-athletes themselves to believe that athletic departments have their academic and personal interests at heart? A small point maybe, but any coach will tell you that attention to detail wins big games.

We athletic coaches and administrators say "education," but we mean "athletics." Despite the high-minded claims that intercollegiate athletics is about education, student-athletes cannot help noticing that athletics is increasingly about entertainment, money, and winning. They see coaches making six figures from lucrative endorsements. They know that 80,000 fans are paying to watch them play football. They note the not-so-subtle messages that are articulated when they are steered to less demanding majors or when NCAA rules are broken in recruiting.

BUSINESS BEFORE EDUCATION

Given inconsistencies like these, it is ironic that the athletic establishment becomes indignant when student-athletes ask to be compensated with a cash stipend over and above their full scholarship. Student-athletes are asking for cash stipends because they have learned what they have been taught by our actions: College athletics is more about money and winning than about books and learning.

A particularly striking example of this inconsistency is the alarm being expressed regarding the increasing number of underclassmen and high school seniors who are leaving school early to turn professional in the sport of basketball. We should be the last people to cry "foul" over this trend. After all, we build athletic programs around maximizing the athletic performance of student-athletes to win games and generate money for athletic department coffers. We recruit prospects based upon athletic ability. From the moment a student-athlete sets foot on campus, he or she begins a training process designed to illicit maximum athletic production. While giving lip service to academic achievement, we emphasize and reward athletic excellence. When a product of such a system develops athletically to a point that precipitates a turn to professional ball, we suddenly begin to voice grave concern over the student-athlete's personal and academic welfare. What else can we expect from a system that is designed to maximize athletic performance?

Concern seems to be less widespread over student-athletes who leave early to play professional baseball. Then again, baseball does not fill 20,000-seat arenas nor does it have the potential to generate a $1.7 billion television contract from CBS to televise its national championship tournament.

But what about loyalty? The college gave the young person a scholarship opportunity. Doesn't he or she owe it to the institution to stay in school? How loyal is the coach who leaves a school at the mere scent of a better contract, shoe deal, or television package? If one of these same student-athletes was an athletic "bust," would his or her scholarship be renewed? If we want to teach them about loyalty, we should award student-athletes a guaranteed four-year scholarship, dependent upon academic performance rather than the current one-year agreement renewable at the sole discretion of the coach. In truth, each student-athlete who completes the one-year contractual obligation to the school has been loyal.

With the emphasis we have placed on athletic competition and the rewards we have given for athletic excellence, how can we argue that education should be the first priority of student-athletes themselves or that they should forfeit a chance at professional ball? One simply has to look at the NCAA's most recent graduation rate report to find that men's basketball student-athletes, and in particular, black basketball student-athletes, are graduating at a rate of only 38 percent (National Collegiate Athletic Association 1996, 622). It's hardly a safe bet to pass up a pro opportunity in exchange for sticking around to obtain a well-rounded college experience or a meaningful degree.

These student-athletes are leaving for one reason: good business. They are simply applying the lessons we have taught them, not with our words, but with our day-to-day actions. Our message has been that college athletics is a business. And student-athletes will continue to leave as long as we persist in placing their athletic development before their academic and personal development, and business before education. Rhetoric about the long-term value of education rings hollow when compared to our short-term "win-at-all-cost" behavior. Student-athletes might not be informed about the specifics of running an athletic department, but they are not dumb. If they are not getting what they were promised when they signed that student-athlete/institutional agreement, they reason it's better to move on to a contract that holds water.

Our actions and decisions on a daily basis are far more important than what we say. If those decisions made and actions taken, from the most mundane administrative detail to the most far-reaching policy decision, do not reflect a commitment to and belief in the value of education, then anything else we say about commitment has no impact whatsoever on the young people in our programs, or on anyone else for that matter. We become educationally irrelevant. To be a contributing member of the higher education community, we cannot be educationally irrelevant.

STUDENT-ATHLETE SUPPORT SERVICES

After reconsidering student-athlete welfare from a philosophical and attitudinal perspective, the next challenge is to provide the programmatic support necessary for student-athletes to succeed academically and socially. Specifically, the purpose, scope, structure, and philosophy of the athletic department's academic support program must be assessed. This seemingly simple task, however, raises some controversial issues.

Providing "special" support services for student-athletes that are not available to the general student body generates substantial criticism from faculty. Such special treatment, it is argued, contributes to student-athletes' difficulty in adjusting to the "real world" after their athletic careers are over. Further, faculty insist that allocating such a disproportionate amount of student services resources to such a small segment of the student body is an example of badly misplaced institutional priorities.

Student-athletes do have special needs, however, that set them apart from the nonathlete. The time and physical demands placed upon them, as well as all the challenges that accompany being highly visible, are unlike those placed upon any other group of students. While the editor of the student newspaper puts in many hours meeting deadlines, none of the activities of publishing a newspaper are as rigorous and physically draining as the violent physical contact demanded by football. Concentrating on schoolwork after crashing your head against a six-foot two-inch, 240-pound linebacker for three hours a day is incredibly difficult. (Imagine having your head slammed in a car door 10 times before going to the library to study for a chemistry test.) Moreover, many student-athletes are "special admissions" to the university, often with significant remedial needs. If the university admits under-prepared student-athletes for the purpose of generating money and exposure, it must also assume responsibility for developing a support system to allow those "special admits" an opportunity to succeed academically and socially.

Faculty concern regarding such special treatment is understandable. Nevertheless, as long as colleges and universities continue to accept student-athletes who are less prepared academically than the general student body and at the same time demand significant amounts of time and effort for peak athletic performance, special academic support programs cannot be termed a luxury; rather they are an institutional responsibility. Comprehensive support programs are one way in which athletic departments can provide student-athletes with a benefit that can improve their chance of earning a meaningful degree and well-balanced academic and social experience. In reality, because student-athletes are generating the money to pay for these special services, they are not being "given" anything.

There is a fine line, however, between meeting the unique needs of student-athletes and treating them as normal students. Academic advisers were first employed in the 1970s with one purpose in mind: to keep student-athletes eligible for competition. Those days, however, are gone. The profession has become much more sophisticated; the support personnel, who were once mostly ex-coaches, take their responsibility as guardians of the welfare of student-athletes more seriously. Student-athlete support personnel are currently trained professionals with advanced degrees in either counseling or student affairs. The result is that the purpose of these programs has changed. Rather than simply to maintain a student-athlete's eligibility, student-athlete support programs are now designed as a vehicle to assist the student-athlete in meeting academic and personal goals. Such programs facilitate the student-athlete's ability to *earn* a quality academic experience, rather than being given one. Universities must remain vigilant to ensure that all campus personnel, including the student-athletes themselves, understand the difference.

One way to underscore the distinction is to remove the student-athlete support program from under direct athletic department control. Most directors of student-athlete support programs report to the athletic director. Such arrangements are clearly not in the best interest of student-athletes. They result in athletic department authority being exercised over the two major facets of the student-athlete's collegiate experience, that is, the athletic component as well as the academic and personal development component. As explained in detail earlier, the conflict between academic and athletic interests is problematic at best; the temptation to compromise academic integrity in favor of athletic eligibility is simply too great. Therefore, the negative effect on both the student-athlete as well as on the credibility of an academic support program that must answer to the athletic department cannot be overemphasized. That being the case, institutions should adjust reporting lines for such programs from the athletic department to the office of student or academic affairs.

STRENGTHENING THE POSITION OF THE DIRECTOR OF STUDENT-ATHLETE SUPPORT PROGRAMS

As previously outlined, student-athlete support program personnel have traditionally been thought of as simply academic advisers and tutors whose main responsibility was to keep student-athletes eligible. As might be expected, the services offered, primarily tutoring and schedule management, reflected this limited view of student-athlete support. Over the last decade, however, such programs have become significantly more comprehensive, evidence of a commitment to the development of the student-athlete in a holistic sense. This change from an eligibility-focused approach to one based upon the development of the total student has resulted in the expansion of the role, responsibilities, and importance of the directors of these programs. It is now necessary to distinguish between the directors and academic advisers, counselors, and tutors.

Academic advisers, counselors, and tutors have a narrow scope of responsibility. However, the directors of student-athlete support programs, particularly at the Division I-A level, oversee a much broader operation. They generally manage a staff of tutors, counselors, and graduate assistants, and they serve as the athletic department's primary liaison to the academic community. With such far-reaching responsibilities, the authority of the director of student-athlete support programs must be strengthened, particularly if an institution is unwilling to transfer its reporting line outside the athletic department. The director must be recognized as a senior staff member and accorded the same authority, prestige, and access to information as the assistant or associate athletic director for business or external affairs. How can an athletic department claim to be "about the student-athlete" when the individual responsible for sports information is accorded higher status than the director of the student-athlete support program?

An example of how directors have not been an integral part of the athletic department decision-making process involves the NCAA's annual appropriation of $25,000 (later raised to $50,000) to each Division I institution specifically for the enhancement of academic support programs. During the initial years in which the money was appropriated (early 1990s), the director of the student-athlete support program was often not consulted by the director of athletics regarding how funds should be used. Of course, that begs the issue of whether at some institutions these monies were used to improve the academic support programs as intended or were simply plowed into the general athletic department budget. Hopefully, directors are now consulted on a regular basis.

Institutions are not the only entities with a responsibility to enhance the position of director of student-athlete support programs. Conference offices can play a significant role in this regard. In an effort to assist institutions in developing comprehensive compliance programs that ensure institutional control over their athletic programs, conference offices were given the charge of supporting, developing, and strengthening the position of institutional compliance coordinator. Consequently, conference resources have been used to coordinate the activities of this important, and still evolving, athletic department position. Conferences need to play a similar role in strengthening the position of the directors of student-athlete support by playing a more active role in raising awareness regarding the importance of such programs and providing support and encouragement for the individual program directors.

As they did with the position of compliance coordinator, conferences should sponsor opportunities for the directors of support programs to meet, share information, and work together to use more effectively the resources that are appropriated in this area. While athletic departments compete, for prospects, fans, and on the fields of play, when it comes to improving compliance efforts and student-athlete support programs, institutions must work together. Conferences have the opportunity and responsibility to support this important component of student-athlete welfare. By providing support, conferences can give much-needed leadership in recognizing the important role directors of student-athlete support programs play in helping athletic departments become "about the student-athlete."

Despite what coaches, athletic directors, or faculty athletic representatives say about knowing what is going on in the lives of their student-athletes, they are not nearly as aware of the issues, challenges, and problems facing student-athletes academically and socially as are the directors of these programs. If you want to find out what is going on in the lives of student-athletes, ask the director of the student-athlete support program. Directors offer a valuable perspective, one that should be considered in making policy at the institutional, conference, and national levels. If college athletics is to be "about the student-athlete," those individuals whose primary responsibility it is to foster the development of student-athletes in a holistic sense must be fully engaged in athletic department and conference decision-making processes.

Now that the athletic department has evaluated and improved where necessary its academic-support program and bolstered the status of the directors of those programs, it is time to give student-athletes a voice in shaping the policies and programs that so greatly affect their lives.

GIVING STUDENT-ATHLETES A VOICE

How can an athletic program be "about the student-athlete" if student-athletes are not asked their thoughts on athletic department and NCAA policies, procedures, or programs? How can student-athletes be empowered when they have virtually no access to the athletic department decision-making process? Coaches, athletic administrators, and faculty athletic representatives have always acted as if they alone know what is best for student-athletes. At times they may know best, but if the opinions of those affected most by NCAA and athletic department policies are not considered, the result may be policy that is out of touch with the needs of the very people those policies are meant to serve.

If college athletics is supposed to be about education, shouldn't student-athletes be provided the opportunity to learn from being involved in a policy-making capacity? "Just play your sport and don't worry about anything else" is the not-so-subtle message sent when student-athletes are excluded from involvement in decision making. It is ironic that we do not think that the same youngsters who are smart enough to quarterback our football teams or run our basketball teams are also capable of having astute observations, clear thoughts, and meaningful suggestions regarding the operation of an athletic program. Not all student-athletes are interested only in playing sports. Many are interested in acquiring the types of leadership skills that are developed through involvement in administrative and policy-making activities. Look at an example from another country.

> In the British boarding schools, sport was governed by the participants. The students organized, managed, and officiated their own sporting events. This was not an anomaly, because self-governance was widely practiced in areas outside of sport as well, but it was particularly important on the playing field. The importance of self-governance lay in the self-conscious way these schools trained the elite for leadership roles in business, industry, government, and the military. It was thought that learning to lead and organize on the playing field would translate into skills useful in other leadership positions. (Shields and Bredemeir 1995, 176-177)

As staff liaison to the Southeastern Conference Student-Athlete Advisory Committee, I was continually amazed at how perceptive, thoughtful, and intelligent student-athletes can be if given the opportunity. They are capable of offering timely and relevant ideas regarding the student-athlete experience. We must provide these young adults with a voice. Then we must listen to that voice . . . very carefully.

Some progress is being made in this area—at least on paper. Over the past few years, institutions and a few conferences have begun to provide student-athletes opportunities to offer feedback regarding issues that concern them. In 1991, the Southeastern Conference was the first to establish a student-athlete advisory committee. The committee has met with much success. For example, the committee's opinion was instrumental in causing the conference to loosen intraconference transfer restrictions, which were much more stringent than the NCAA's. In fact, the way in which this change played out illustrated how such committees can make a difference. After the student-athlete committee proposed the change, various constituent groups within the conference had an opportunity to review and discuss the issue before the proposal was submitted to the conference presidents for a binding vote. While the student-athletes and faculty athletic representatives supported the change, the athletic directors were adamantly opposed. When the presidents heard both sides of the issue, they voted with the student-athletes to loosen the transfer restrictions. Without a student-athlete advisory committee, the issue would never have appeared on the conference agenda.

The committee has also had success on the national level. It was the originator of legislation sponsored in 1995 by the Special Committee to Review Student-Athlete Welfare, Access and Equity that added student-athlete representatives to various NCAA committees. It was also the driving force behind the SEC's sponsoring of a resolution at the 1993 NCAA Convention asking the NCAA Council and Presidents Commission to consider requiring all institutions to form a student-athlete advisory committee. The resolution was adopted, and two years later legislation was passed mandating the establishment of such committees at all NCAA institutions.

To comply with the NCAA rule, an institution must establish a student-athlete committee. However, to meet the intent of the legislation, the committee should be an active, working committee with real authority—one that is provided access to pertinent information, such as budget figures and departmental policies. How does an institution make such a committee work?

The following are suggestions for making student-athlete committees more than simply window dressing.

1. *Representation from outside the athletic department.* Student-athletes are concerned with both athletic and nonathletic matters. Therefore, a representative from outside the athletic department, say from the Dean of Students Office or the Minority Affairs Office, should be on the committee to offer nonathletic opinions and observations. Given the propensity for athletic department officials to be concerned primarily with the student-athletes' athletic welfare, an outside "check" must be

in place to assure that student-athletes' nonathletic concerns are addressed adequately.

2. *A committed athletic department liaison.* It takes hard work and a genuine commitment from a senior athletic department administrator to make student-athlete committees effective. Gathering information, framing issues, tracking trends, and following up on the committee's recommendations demand diligence and persistence. Student-athletes are not in a position to compile such information and track their recommendations through the various committees and policy-making bodies. This legwork must be performed by the administrative liaison. The administrative liaison must also be an effective advocate for student-athlete issues and rights. He or she must be willing to present the student-athletes' viewpoints, regardless of how unpopular they are within the athletic department. Finally, this administrative responsibility should be a formal component of the liaison's job description, not simply an "add-on" responsibility, and should be considered in his or her performance evaluation.

3. *Committees that represent a wide diversity of student-athletes in the program.* Institutions must resist the temptation to place only the best and brightest of student-athletes on committees. Not only should straight-A students be on the committee, so should students who are struggling academically. Obviously, diversity in the areas of gender, race, and sport should be sought. One of the major criticisms of student-athlete committees is that they often do not represent the true diversity of the student-athlete population, particularly as it relates to academic achievement.

Thus, to most effectively serve the interests of student-athletes and the athletic department, the goal should not be to appoint the most impressive committee, but rather the committee most representative of the student-athlete population.

4. *Coaches should not assign representatives.* Committee representatives should be determined by the students themselves, rather than by coaches. Student-athlete advisory committees are intended to represent the concerns of students and not, by proxy, the coaches.

5. *Faculty athletic representative involvement.* The institution's faculty athletic representative should be an active member of the committee. The faculty athletic representative is charged with safeguarding the integrity of the student-athlete experience. Interacting with student-athletes on such committees will keep the faculty athletic representative in touch with the needs of student-athletes and will help in his or her role as an advocate for student-athlete rights and welfare.

6. *Communicating results.* The minutes of committee meetings should be circulated to various campus constituencies. For example, the faculty senate athletic committee, university president, the dean of students,

and all athletic department members should be made aware of the recommendations and actions of the committee.

7. *Committee representatives' involvement in other athletic department policy-making bodies.* Representatives from the student-athlete committee should also serve on all other athletic department policy boards and committees. Such inclusion will facilitate effective communication between the student-athletes and the relevant policy-making bodies. Additionally, a student-athlete committee representative should be included on search committees for coaches.

Institutional and conference student-athlete committees can provide student-athletes a clear voice in formulating the policies and procedures that so greatly affect their lives. If there is an institutional commitment to making them viable, working bodies, the committees can have a great impact on student-athlete welfare and can go a long way in making an athletic program "about the student-athlete."

THE NECESSITY OF NATIONAL STUDENT-ATHLETE INPUT

In November 1995, I attended a national symposium sponsored by Northeastern University's Center for Study of Sport. The day's focus was student-athlete welfare. One session, featuring four recently graduated student-athletes who discussed their views on intercollegiate athletics, served to illustrate how perceptive and thoughtful student-athletes can be if given the opportunity to express their viewpoints freely.

The discussion began with a tremendously powerful but equally disheartening story told by a former quarterback. He related the story of his last play as a college student-athlete and vividly described standing in the pocket and firing a pass toward the sideline. His voice grew more passive as he told of the pass being intercepted and returned by the opposing team for a touchdown. What was most disturbing was the deflated way in which he told the group that at that point he could not have cared less about the interception, the ensuing loss, and the end of his college athletic career. "The game was no longer fun," he said. "They killed all the love I had for it." Then a former track student-athlete told of being pressured to return from an injury sooner than her body was telling her she should. Still another student, an African American, told of his feelings of isolation on what was an overwhelmingly white campus.

The panelists then began to discuss the need for student-athletes to have a voice in the various decision- and policy-making processes at both the institutional and national levels. Particular attention was paid to the failure of the NCAA to incorporate a meaningful mechanism for student-athlete input into its restructuring proposal that was to be voted upon during the upcoming January 1996 convention. This story prompted the former quarterback to liken student-athletes' status within the NCAA to that of a Third World country. He pointed out that in most of the world's governing agencies, such as the World Bank or the United Nations, the countries with the largest GNP or greatest military power control the vote. Third World countries, he continued, are, for the most part, not heard from, and more often than not, they are simply viewed as pawns in world power politics.

The symposium dialogue began to take a harder edge as various athletic administrators in the audience, some of them senior-ranking NCAA officials, were challenged to respond to the student-athletes' concerns. Unfortunately, their responses, while well intentioned, served only to highlight just how far removed from reality athletic administrators are in their perceptions and understanding of today's student-athlete experience. For example, more than one administrator indicated that a formalized mechanism for student-athlete input at the national level was largely unnecessary. Student-athlete concerns, this group said, should be voiced and addressed at the institutional level. But in the minds of the panelists, a student-athlete voicing concern about a coach's overemphasis on athletics, gender or racial discrimination, or questionable ethical behavior would most likely be labeled a "bad apple" or a "malcontent." A student-athlete who criticizes his or her athletic program runs the risk of quickly becoming an expendable cog of the athletic machine, for many coaches feel that student-athletes who are not eternally and uncompromisingly loyal to the program do not deserve to have their annual scholarship renewed.

The reality of the situation for student-athletes is that at the institutional level they can voice only limited concerns in limited ways. Regardless of whether this is true, the fact that they believe it to be the truth is what makes it imperative that there be a meaningful vehicle for student-athlete input at the national level. Issues that must be addressed both on campus as well as in a national forum are the relationship between student-athlete and coach; coaches' responsibilities as educators; the win-at-all-cost philosophy; and the student-athlete's right to be provided a legitimate opportunity to earn a well-balanced academic, social, and athletic experience. National dialogue serves to raise awareness and to spur action at the local level.

I want to relate a glaring example of how far removed we can be from issues affecting student-athletes. When a long-time administrator expressed dismay that student-athletes were criticizing their athletic experience, he proceeded to tell his listeners about his wonderful experience as a student-athlete . . . in the 1950s! His comments graphically illustrated why college athletics has lost its focus. The issues being discussed on this day had nothing to do with his experience in the 1950s or my experience in the 1970s. Although we should draw upon our experiences as former student-athletes, current student-athletes are concerned with the issues *they* are facing *now . . . today.*

That interchange provided all the evidence necessary for the need to include as part of the newly restructured NCAA a direct line of communication from student-athletes to presidents. Currently, the Division I student-athlete committee reports to a management council consisting of athletic directors, conference commissioners, senior women administrators, and faculty athletic representatives. This management council reports to a board of directors consisting of presidents. While well intentioned, this structure is inadequate. As the panel discussion illustrated (and my experience with the SEC student-athlete committee confirmed), student-athlete viewpoints, particularly negative ones, are all too often trivialized by athletic administrators and dismissed as the ungrateful grumblings of malcontents. Thus, the Division I student-athlete advisory committees, as well as those of Divisions II and III in the NCAA, should be provided a direct line of access to their divisional president's board.

Rather than being marginalized as "bad apples," student-athletes who voice their concerns in a responsible fashion should be celebrated as being courageous enough to stand up for something they believe in. Each of the panelists that day would tell you that they believe in the student-athlete experience, but only if it is kept in the proper perspective. During recruitment, and often thereafter, they were told that college athletics was about them—and they believed it. They bought into the ideal that college athletics was about education, the love of the game, and the opportunity to earn a well-balanced academic, social, and athletic experience. Now, after it is over, they wonder what went wrong. It is their belief in the student-athlete ideal, not any desire to tear down or destroy college athletics, that prompts them to speak out; they simply want to make the system better for those who will follow. If the NCAA is to be "about the student-athlete," it must always provide student-athletes with a strong, clear, and unfiltered vehicle for direct input to the presidents.

EXIT INTERVIEWS

Another way to provide opportunities for student-athlete input is through the NCAA mandated exit interview program. NCAA legislation requires the institution's director of athletics, senior woman administrator, or designated representatives to conduct exit interviews in each sport with a sampling of student-athletes whose eligibility has expired. NCAA legislation does not, however, specify a program format, nor does it evaluate such programs. Such being the case, their scope and effectiveness varies greatly among institutions. But again, while well intentioned in principle, this NCAA initiative falls short of what is necessary to maximize student-athletes' opportunities for meaningful input at the institutional level.

At most institutions, the athletic department has set up its student-athlete exit interview program. Simply put, most athletic department personnel know little about student retention and how to make such programs effective. Regardless, student-athlete exit interview programs are developed without consulting with institutional experts on student retention, usually housed in the student services area. Over the last 15 years, institutional research aimed at identifying reasons for student attrition as well as institutional programming to improve retention rates have increased significantly. In short, institutions have a greater understanding of why students leave school and how to increase those students' chances of staying in school than anyone in the athletic department. Unfortunately, athletic departments persistently refuse to reach out to these institutional experts to develop an effective exit interview program. Instead, most interview programs consist of either a questionnaire or an opportunity for the exiting student-athlete to interview with the athletic director or another athletic department official.

If the athletic department were to tap into its university expertise, it would discover that student retention research indicates that interviewing student-athletes as they leave the institution is simply too late.

> Especially important to the process of departure are the stages of separation and transition to college. Since these are normally experienced very early in the student career, typically during the first semester and year of college life, more emphasis should be placed on the collection of information about the quality of student experiences during the early, rather than later, stages of association with the institution. As in the case of pre-entry data, early data collection leaves open the possibility that actions can be taken to remedy problems before they result in withdrawal. (Tinto 1993, 220-221)

Athletic departments need to devise a program for conducting interviews of randomly selected groups of students from all classes. The current NCAA provision could be amended to stipulate that the institution interview at least 10 percent of its underclass student-athletes annually. Student-athletes who may actually experience the changes they suggest are far more likely to devote thoughtful attention to such interviews. Further, if student-athletes are experiencing difficulties, they can be identified before it is too late.

Institutional experts in student retention would also be able to tell athletic department officials that "since the most dissatisfied leavers are least likely to respond to such surveys, the picture one obtains of 'reasons for leaving' is highly skewed toward the less negative. It is for this reason and many others that survey methods are best used in situations where incentives exist or can be applied to heighten response rates (e.g., use of a lottery) and where follow-up methods (e.g., telephone interviews) can be employed to ascertain the views of a representative sample of survey nonrespondents" (Tinto 1993, 217).

Athletic directors would also learn that rather than interviewing student-athletes themselves, both their interests and those of their student-athletes would be better served by using trained student interviewers. "All too often insensitive or highly structured, directed questioning of students leads to self-fulfilling results which produce findings that serve more to reinforce prior institutional expectations than to accurately mirror strongly held student views. In this instance, trained student interviewers are often more effective than faculty or staff. . . . In part, their power arises from the fact that student observers are less inclined than adult observers to filter their observations through the sometimes biased lenses that are used by institutional representatives" (Tinto 1993, 218).

Finally, interview results should be compiled and circulated to various campus constituencies. Making certain such information is widely distributed is an excellent way to better inform the university community that the athletic department has nothing to hide from the academic community. Interview results should be circulated to any athletic policy-making board, including the faculty senate athletic committee, the president, the faculty athletic representative, the dean of students, and the student-athlete committee.

A case can be made that the athletic department should not be responsible for the exit interview program. Inasmuch as institutional expertise and resources to conduct effective interview programs are far greater than the athletic department's, coupled with the fact that many of the issues student-athletes are concerned with relate to student life rather than strictly athletics, serious consideration should be given to amending this NCAA rule to specify that the responsibility for conducting such a program rests with the institution rather than the athletic department.

Again, while well intentioned, the athletic community's efforts regarding this student-athlete welfare initiative fall short. They fall short largely because the athletic department is divorced from the rest of the campus community and unwilling to reach out to build the necessary bridges that will benefit student-athletes in their academic and personal development. In this area, the athletic department must reach out to the academic community for the benefit of the student-athlete. Contrary to the prevailing mind-set of many athletic departments, the "other side of campus" is not the enemy.

As with the student-athlete committee, an athletic department, if it is truly committed to being "about the student-athlete," can use an exit-interview program as an excellent vehicle to provide student-athletes a voice in shaping the policies that influence their lives and also as a valuable tool for increasing student-athlete retention, thereby improving graduation rates. But again, it takes commitment, hard work, and a willingness to reach out to the academic community if we are to realize this goal.

STUDENT-ATHLETE WELFARE AS PART OF INSTITUTIONAL CONTROL

Over the past 10 years, the NCAA has spent a significant amount of time and resources defining and emphasizing its concept of institutional control. "It is the responsibility of each member institution to control its intercollegiate athletics program in compliance with the rules and regulations of the Association," reads the NCAA Constitution, Article 2.2.1 (National Collegiate Athletic Association 1996, 3). As might be expected, the focus of the NCAA's efforts has been to help institutions develop systems of checks and balances to ensure that athletic department personnel comply with its rules.

For example, if coaches are to be expected to know and abide by NCAA recruiting rules, educational programs must be established to teach them those rules. Compliance systems have been developed to ensure the proper certification of student-athletes in the areas of financial aid and eligibility. Finally, institutional control efforts have focused upon ensuring an appropriate level of presidential authority and oversight of athletic programs. Regrettably, the issue of student-athlete welfare has not been included as part of the NCAA's institutional control debate as these efforts have focused almost exclusively on enhancing presidential authority and controlling violations of specific NCAA rules in the areas of recruiting, financial aid, playing and practice seasons, and eligibility.

For our athletic departments to "be about the student-athlete," the NCAA must expand its vision of institutional control to include student-athlete welfare. Wilford Bailey and Taylor Littleton in *Athletics and Academe: An Anatomy of Abuses and a Prescription for Reform* correctly identify the lack of appropriate institutional attention to or control over student-athlete welfare as one of three primary forms of "abuse" in intercollegiate athletics. Their point, an extremely provocative one, is that the abdication of institutional responsibility for student-athlete welfare is every bit as much of an "abuse" or "violation" as a coach breaking a recruiting rule or an institution not having in place an adequate system to monitor eligibility (Bailey and Littleton 1991, xi).

Emphasizing specific rules and establishing effective compliance systems are no doubt important. However, institutional efforts must not only emphasize compliance with specific NCAA rules, they must also comply with the broader principles of the Association. We must make the understanding of these broad principles an institutional priority. They must be emphasized at every opportunity, for they represent the foundation upon which all institutional control discussions and initiatives should be based. If more is done to help coaches, administrators, boosters, media, and student-athletes understand and appreciate these broad principles, particularly those relating to student-athlete welfare, compliance with the specifics will be more likely to occur.

The NCAA's 20-hour-per-week practice limitation offers an excellent example of how this approach to institutional control can improve student-athlete welfare. Currently, coaches and student-athletes are informed of the specific rule and institutional compliance coordinators monitor its compliance by asking student-athletes to sign time sheets verifying adherence to the rule. In actuality, student-athletes are simply told to sign these sheets, knowing full well that in many cases they have practiced well beyond the 20-hour limit. Such blatant disregard for a rule that is so central to the principle of student-athlete welfare cannot be tolerated.

The only way in which principles of student-athlete welfare will be honored is if student-athletes are informed of the rule and their fundamental right to earn a well-balanced academic, social, and athletic experience. Further, they need to know that they have the right to hold coaches accountable for compromising those principles. Finally, and most important, they must know that the NCAA will enforce the rule.

While institutional efforts will raise the awareness of the link between adherence with this rule and its effect on student-athlete welfare, the NCAA Committee on Infractions must raise the stakes for its violation. To that end, the Committee must begin to process and penalize institutions that violate this particular rule. Further, student-athletes must be provided assurances that if they voice such concerns, their confidentiality will not be violated. The result will be that coaches will begin to understand that their institution and the NCAA take the principle of student-athlete welfare seriously and that they will be held accountable for compliance not only with the specific rule but also with the broader principle that it affects.

Committee members will argue that it is difficult to identify, process, and penalize an institution for such a vague concept. The principles of student-athlete welfare, however, are no less vague than the principle of institutional control was only a few years ago. Defining and processing violations of institutional control is an ongoing process. Once the NCAA determined that universities must be responsible for ensuring effective institutional control over their athletic departments, the committee began the process of defining its elements and developing standards and expectations for its implementation. A similar effort and commitment from the NCAA as it applies to student-athlete welfare is not only necessary but reasonable and achievable.

The legislative mandate for the committee to address this issue is clear. Not only does Article 2.2 of the NCAA Constitution outline these "Principles of Student-Athlete Welfare" (notably the second of the NCAA's "Principles for Conduct of Intercollegiate Athletics," immediately following the "Principle of Institutional Control and Responsibility"), NCAA Constitution, Article 1.3, identifies as a "Fundamental Policy" of the association to "maintain intercollegiate athletics as an integral part of the educational program and the athlete as an integral part of the student body" (National Collegiate Athletic Association 1996, 1).

If our athletic programs are to be "about the student-athlete," student-athlete welfare must be considered a component of institutional control expectations. Approaching the concept of student-athlete welfare in this way will force athletic department personnel to adopt a framework for decision making that is centered on the student-athlete. Student-athlete welfare is not a stand-alone issue. It is a fundamental institutional responsibility and just as much a part of institutional control as a system to monitor recruiting.

OUR PRODUCT IS THE STUDENT-ATHLETE

Being honest with student-athletes about the realities of major college athletics; providing them more autonomy to make their own decisions; giving them a "voice"; and incorporating student-athlete welfare as a component of institutional control are all suggestions that can contribute to making the student-athlete/institutional agreement a fair one. They are all achievable goals provided we focus upon what is in the best interests of the young people in our athletic programs for the next 50 years of their lives rather than solely upon winning next week's game.

Making our programs "about the student-athlete" is not only the right thing to do, it is also good business. Taking care of "your people," whether it be in a company as large as General Motors or as small as the mom-and-pop grocery store on the corner, results in greater "worker" loyalty and productivity. The long-term benefits of sending well-rounded graduates who remember their college athletic experience as one in which they were treated fairly, honestly, and with dignity will last for years to come. Former student-athletes all visit their hometowns. They will all interact with a wide range of people, including future prospects for the institution and their parents, alumni, and even corporate executives. They will all talk about their intercollegiate athletic experience, and hopefully they will one day be in the position to contribute money to the institution.

While some may think that our product is the game itself, the only products we produce that have potential for significant lasting impact are the young people who participate in our programs. If we send good human beings into the world, they will speak kindly of our programs and reflect well upon them. Making a commitment to conduct an athletic program that is truly "about the student-athlete" and unquestionably has at its center the student-athlete's long-term academic and personal well-being is a sound business investment.

To meet our end of the student-athlete/institutional agreement, we must not be afraid to empower student-athletes. If the goal of athletic participation is to prepare student-athletes for life after athletics, we must not exert so much control over their lives that they leave the university with a world view that stretches no further than the locker room. The ability to succeed in the game of life depends on how functional an individual is in a nonathletic culture. Athletic stardom opens a few doors for student-athletes; whether they are able to step through those doors and make the most of their opportunities depends on their ability to deal with real-world challenges. To help bring that about is *our* challenge.

References

Bailey, Wilford S., and Taylor D. Littleton. 1991. *Athletics and Academe: An Anatomy of Abuses and a Prescription for Reform.* New York: Macmillan.

Kjeldsen, Eric. 1992. "The Manager's Role in the Development and Maintenance of Ethical Behavior in the Sport Organization." *Journal of Sport Management* 6.

National Collegiate Athletic Association. 1996. *1996 NCAA Division I Graduation-Rates Report.* Overland Park, KS: NCAA.

National Collegiate Athletic Association. 1988. *Studies of Intercollegiate Athletics.* Report No. 1. Palo Alto, CA: American Institutes for Research.

Shields, David, and Brenda Bredemeir. 1995. *Character Development and Physical Activity.* Champaign, IL: Human Kinetics.

Tinto, Vincent. 1993. *Leaving College: Rethinking the Causes and Cures of Student Attrition.* Chicago: The University of Chicago Press.

CHAPTER 6

The Coach as Educator

There is no subject more worthy of the attention of political leaders at any level than the education of our children and the preparation of those who teach them.

Thomas H. Kean
Thinking About American Higher Education

At the time athletics was formally incorporated into higher education, coaches were usually faculty members who were also given coaching assignments. Athletics was an extracurricular activity for both the students and the English professor who coached them. But as public interest in college athletics grew and its potential as a revenue-generating enterprise increased, institutions began to employ full-time professional coaches. This fundamental change in the coaching profile has not stopped those in the athletic community from continuing to insist that coaches are, before all else, educators. The playing field or court, they insist, is a coach's classroom, and the lessons taught there in discipline, teamwork, and sportsmanship are just as important as the lessons being taught in the lecture hall or the chemistry lab.

The realities of major college athletics, however, suggest otherwise. Coaches are neither hired nor evaluated based upon their commitment to higher education. In today's high-pressure world of college athletics, coaches, particularly in the sports of football and basketball, are hired and fired based upon their ability to produce winning teams that generate revenue.

As a result, whether or not it is deserved, coaches are viewed as slick-looking, fast-talking entertainers and entrepreneurs rather than as educators, men and women far more concerned about winning games than about graduating student-athletes. They are largely viewed as having little connection to the educational community. The "coach as educator" ideal has gone the way of the leather football helmet. George Blaney, former head basketball coach at Holy Cross and at Seton Hall University and former president of the National Association of Basketball Coaches (NABC), summed up the coaches' loss of credibility in the following manner: "It was our [the coaches'] fault we lost the public's [trust] because of violations and abuses. Getting back that esteem from administrators and the public is what we are striving for, to consider us as educator-coaches" (Blaney 1993, C-1). We now ask ourselves what has brought about such a dramatic change in the coaching model? And what can be done to restore it?

CHANGING MOTIVATION FOR COACHING

Arguably, the college coach's job description has changed more in the last 25 years than any other job description in the higher education community. Most Division I football and basketball coaches will agree that the actual teaching and coaching of their sport as well as their involvement in the off-the-field interests of their student-athletes occupies an increasingly smaller percentage of their time. Coaches are now the most recognized personalities on campus and thus have been asked to be more involved in university-wide fund-raising and public relations efforts. The pressure for coaches to win and at the same time be accessible to the media has also increased dramatically. Finally, many coaches have become full-fledged entrepreneurs with their own television and radio shows, summer camps, shoe contracts, and endorsements.

The evolution of the recruiting process has also affected significant change in the "coach as educator" ideal. Before recruiting became a highly sophisticated and international operation, much of it was happenstance. Prospects heard about athletic programs through newspapers, letters, phone calls, and by word of mouth. A loose network of alumni and talent scouts identified and performed most of the face-to-face off-campus recruiting. In the 1930s for example, Northwestern University appointed almost 50 "alumni counselors" to scout for football prospects (Lester 1995, 137). In some cases, a prospect might show up on campus without any recruitment. How that has changed! Recruiting is now looked upon as the lifeblood of a program because coaches understand that they will not win many games with only mediocre talent. Thus, considerable time and money are spent recruiting prospects worldwide.

This increased emphasis on recruiting has resulted in a shift in the desired credentials for and backgrounds of assistant coaches. Thirty years ago the most important hiring criteria for an assistant coach were his or her teaching ability and coaching experience. Head coaches at the college level looked for experienced assistants who were committed educators. Candidates with those credentials were usually found in high schools, which were filled with head coaches with master's degrees and years of classroom experience.

Today, the most important characteristics an assistant coach must possess are the personality and ability to sell the program to 17- and 18-year-old high school All-Americans. "You recruit 'em and I'll coach 'em," orders the head coach. If an assistant coach cannot deliver top-notch talent on a consistent basis, he or she will not be an assistant coach for long. The result is that the qualities and background of a committed educator are simply no longer a valued component of an assistant coach's credentials.

Many highly qualified high school head coaches, particularly veteran coaches with families, are reluctant to become college assistant coaches because of the travel required. Further, after experiencing the hands-on coaching and decision-making responsibility required of a head coach, high school coaches do not have much interest in simply becoming recruiters at the college level. The result is that there are fewer college coaches cast in the traditional "coach as educator" mold as an increasing number of coaches are entering the college ranks immediately after their playing days are over.

Some say that the motive for entering the profession has changed. Young people once entered coaching because they loved the game and were committed to using sports as a vehicle to teach. Coaches certainly did not coach to get rich. My father has been a high school coach for 46 years. In 1950 he earned $100 as an assistant baseball coach, $150 as an assistant football coach, and $400 as the head basketball coach. As a head football coach from 1955 to 1973, he never earned more than $2,400. Currently, he earns $4,200 a year as an assistant football coach.

After serving for seven years as a high school teacher and coach, Bo Brickels, my former coach at Davidson, earned $6,000 as an assistant coach at Rice University in 1967. He was also required to teach a few courses. Most head coaches during that time were earning from $12,000 to $15,000 per year. Many taught or had summer jobs to supplement their incomes.

College coaching today, however, offers the opportunity not only to become wealthy, but also to become a national celebrity. Head coaches often command salary "packages" worth hundreds of thousands of dollars.

Even key assistant coaches can earn a six-figure income. These packages include endorsement opportunities, shoe contracts, appearances on television shows or shows of their own, and income from summer camps. With games being televised nationally, a coach can quickly become a media star. Could it be that young people are entering the coaching profession for different reasons than 30 years ago? Could it be that the possibility of significant compensation as well as national celebrity status attracts a different individual to college coaching? As a result of this change in status, have we placed student-athletes in the hands of coaches who have more interest in getting rich and becoming celebrities than in education?

One of my most disheartening moments at the Southeastern Conference occurred over the issue of how coaches perceive themselves. The conference conducted a series of diversity training workshops for athletic personnel at each conference school. One of the workshop exercises involved compiling a list of personal descriptors, such as "white," "female," "married," "Southerner," or "administrator." The workshop leaders then called out a few of the descriptors, asking anyone in the audience who identified with a particular descriptor to stand. The purpose of the exercise was to demonstrate that it is far more difficult to stand in front of a large group if you are the only person the descriptor applies to than it is when you are one of 10 or 20 people to which the descriptor applies. I was dismayed when the workshop leader asked that any person who identified with the term "educator" stand up. Invariably, only about half of any group stood up. Those who did not stand either did not understand the exercise or simply did not view themselves as educators. To be involved in college athletics either as a coach or an administrator and not to consider yourself to be first and foremost an educator is, frankly, inexcusable.

Before proceeding, reference must be made to the fact that many of the points presented regarding coaches as educators apply to athletic administrators as well. Similar to the shift in the desired credentials of coaches is a growing trend to hire athletic directors with strong business credentials that, in many cases, have been compiled outside the academic community. An informal survey of Division I-A college presidents conducted by the executive search firm of Eastman and Beaudine and reported in the *NCAA News* revealed characteristics that presidents seek in athletic directors.

- Strategic Thinking—the ability to develop, evaluate, and implement short- and long-term plans.
- Knowledge of and sensitivity to gender equity issues and regulatory procedures.
- Ability to manage complex financial issues and budgets.
- Capability to direct a large and diverse staff, including coaches.
- Marketing expertise.

- Strong public speaking, writing, and media relations skills.
- Creativity and problem-solving abilities.
- Effective human resource talents for dealing with parents, students, faculty, booster groups, and sponsors. (Eastman and Beaudine, 1994, 13)

Incredibly, this list of desired credentials mentions neither academic background nor achievement; neither is there an appreciation for nor an understanding of the role of athletics within higher education and the ability to function within that environment. While it is important for an athletic director to possess the business acumen to balance a budget, one has to wonder what effect such a trend is having on the educational priorities of athletic programs, and, in particular, on the academic and personal welfare of student-athletes. The focus of this chapter will be on coaches and their role as educators because they are the ones who have the most hands-on, day-to-day contact with the student-athlete. But the fact remains that each and every member of an athletic department's staff has responsibilities as an educator, which makes the principles suggested in this chapter applicable to administrators as well as coaches.

EDUCATIONAL RESPONSIBILITIES

For whatever reasons, many coaches have come to trivialize their responsibilities as academic and personal role models. This is particularly true in the area of academics. The increased emphasis on the development of quality academic support programs has been taken as a sign by some coaches that the responsibility for the academic and personal development of student-athletes rests solely with the academic support staff. Further, many coaches, citing as their justification the intense pressure to produce winning teams, have come to believe that their only responsibility is for their team's on-the-field performance. Regardless, coaches continue to have a significant influence over student-athletes not only in athletic matters but also in personal and academic affairs. Many coaches justify this indifference to their academic responsibilities by arguing that student-athletes are far better off simply for having spent time on a college campus. To their way of thinking, it does not matter how long a student has been in school or whether he or she ends up with a degree. Ultimately, they argue, it is up to the student-athlete to earn the degree. One former Southeastern Conference basketball coach regularly made this point as follows: "Do you want to know what kids graduate? Those who want to." Unfortunately, it is not that simple.

While there is a measure of truth to this claim, it is particularly troublesome for a coach or any other educational leader to think in such limited terms. Undoubtedly, student-athletes must assume responsibility for their academic and personal experience, but inherent in that coach's comment is a complete abdication of responsibility for anything other than the student-athlete's athletic welfare. If coaches are going to continue to justify their place on a college campus by claiming they are educators, and if they are going to claim that participation in college athletics has educational value, they need to take responsibility for their roles as educators. To wash one's hands of all educational accountability is simply irresponsible; it is even more reprehensible after having sat in a prospect's livingroom during recruitment and made an unqualified pledge to assist him or her in earning a degree.

It is important to note that concern regarding the quality of teaching on the college campus is not limited to coaches. Faculty are also being criticized for having lost sight of their fundamental responsibilities as teachers. Similar to coaches being criticized for pursuing outside endorsement contracts and speaking engagements, faculty are under fire for spending too much time and effort securing outside consulting contracts or in applying for grants to conduct research. In both cases, those who suffer from this apparent neglect of teaching and mentoring responsibilities are the students.

Most calls for higher education reform include the reengagement of faculty with teaching. "Consequently, faculty development programs are on the rise, as are the numbers of research studies and books on improving post-secondary teaching and learning. Forty-four percent of four-year institutions report some type of formal faculty development programs, and an increasing number of foundations and research centers are also involved in meeting this need" (Gilley 1991, 56).

Concern regarding the importance of education and the need for well-trained, competent teachers, however, stretches far beyond American college campuses. These are issues of global significance. "In this world there is no literate population that is poor, no illiterate population that is not," writes John Kenneth Galbraith in *The Good Society: The Humane Agenda*. "Where there is internal peace and passably effective government," he continues, "the primary emphasis must be on education. For that, money must be generously available—money for schools, equipment and teachers, and especially for the training of teachers" (Galbraith 1996, 133-34).

The place of coaches on campus has been justified by claiming that they are teachers and educators. However, many people within academe and in the general public question whether coaches are fulfilling their educational and mentoring responsibilities. Worse, some coaches believe they bear little responsibility for the academic and personal development of their student-athletes. If we are to achieve the New Standard, the "coach as educator" model must be restored. What, then, can the higher education community do to reestablish the "coach as educator" ideal?

REDEFINING THE EXPECTATIONS OF THE COACH

The first step in restoring the "coach as educator" ideal is to begin to discuss and identify the expectations, responsibilities, and desired behaviors of coaches. What is a coach? What credentials should a coach posses? How should a competent coach act? What are the responsibilities of a coach?

Those who consider the effort to answer these questions fruitless are selling coaches short. Coaches are far more flexible and reasonable than they are given credit for. If their expectations are clearly identified by presidents and the academic community, they can be expected, as products of the authoritarian athletic culture, to respond to those expectations. Coaches understand authority. Coaches have been trained to respond to authority figures, which in their case have been coaches they have played under throughout their own years as athletes. If expectations are clear, coaches will meet them. But regardless of whether you think coaches can meet such changing expectations, one thing is certain. There is absolutely no chance of reestablishing the "coach as educator" ideal until expectations are clearly defined. So what are those expectations?

First, coaches must be made to understand fully the responsibility they bear as a tremendously influential person in the life of the student-athlete. According to the results of the 1987-88 NCAA *National Study of Intercollegiate Athletes*, 55 percent of all football and basketball student-athletes reported that their college coach was an important influence on their educational or career plans. In other sports, 49 percent reported the coach as being an important influence. The report also revealed that only 36 percent of students in other extracurricular activities felt that the directors of those extracurricular activities were an important influence on their education or career plans (National Collegiate Athletic Association 1988, 15). With such influence comes responsibility.

Coaches must be held more accountable for providing the necessary support and encouragement to allow the student-athlete to perform successfully in all matters academic and personal. Coaches have the power to set the tone of their programs and to strike the balance between athletics and academics. Coaches need to become more active in creating an environment within their programs that is conducive to the positive academic and social development of their student-athletes. While the quality of an athletic department's student-athlete support program plays an important part in helping all student-athletes, especially those at risk, coaches are ultimately in the best position to influence student-athlete performance in the classroom. Coaches control playing time. And all coaches know that student-athletes, when challenged, will perform. This is particularly true if their performance, whether it be academic, social, or athletic, directly relates to playing time.

Coaches must also be held more responsible for promoting the basic ethical values of honesty and fair play. After all, coaches claim that participation in athletics teaches sportsmanship and fair play. And aren't coaches the teachers on the athletic playing fields and courts? Cheating, whether breaking recruiting rules, bending the rules of play, or displaying unsportsmanlike sideline behavior can simply no longer be tolerated. The responsibility for promoting honesty and fair play applies not only to coaches but to administrators as well. Athletic directors often adopt a "don't ask, don't know" approach to their oversight of their coaches' programs, particularly if the coach is powerful and popular. But regardless of the coach's power or popularity, athletic directors must fully exercise their oversight responsibilities. Some things are worth losing your job over. Promoting ethical responsibility and protecting the academic integrity of the institution are two worthy reasons.

The opportunity and responsibility to teach these valuable lessons is no longer limited to the student-athletes on the team; a coach's influence extends far beyond the campus. Due to widespread media coverage, particularly the increasing television coverage of college athletic events, coaches have much bigger "classrooms" in which to teach. Given the nature of their position, coaches more than any others, with the possible exception of politicians, can influence societal attitudes and behavior as they relate to issues of sportsmanship, fairness, and ethics. But even in the case of politicians, television ratings for the Final Four games and even most college football games dwarf those of C-Span's coverage of congressional committee hearings. Along with the increased fame and fortune that comes with such television exposure, comes increased responsibility. Regardless of whether this added burden is right or fair, it is reality. Coaches must fully understand their far-ranging and ever-increasing educational responsibilities.

This reality was brought home to me while working for the Southeastern Conference. In an effort to increase communication between the conference office and the state high school athletic associations in the states in which an SEC school was located, the directors of those state associations were invited to Birmingham for a brainstorming session. One of the questions posed to the directors was whether the professionalism and caliber of their coaches was improving. The answer was a resounding, "No!" Most disturbing, however, was the reason given for why high school coaches are increasingly difficult to manage. Each of the directors cited the influence of college coaches, particularly in the area of bench conduct and decorum, as the major cause of the decline in sportsmanship and professionalism among high school coaches. As one director put it, "Who do you think our coaches are modeling themselves after? They are watching *your* coaches on television!"

According to Charles Breithaupt of Texas's statewide University Interscholastic League, "Young coaches watch the great ones 'working' officials. They see how it's successful and entertaining. But they have to consider they have 14- and 15-year-olds on the bench and conduct themselves with that in mind" (Lipsyte 1997, sec. 8, p. 4).

The NCAA has begun an effort to highlight the principles of sportsmanship and fair play. However, most attention has been placed upon the on-the-field behavior of student-athletes. For example, student-athletes in football are now being penalized for any celebratory behavior judged to be excessive or for behavior that draws attention to the individual. Coaches and administrators correctly argue that excessive "showboating" compromises the principles of good sportsmanship. But the fundamental principle of good sportsmanship is fairness and honesty. Could it be that student-athletes are applying the lessons learned from observing coaches breaking recruiting rules, running practices in excess of the NCAA limit of 20 hours per week, or telling student-athletes to do anything on the field to "get the job done . . . just do not let an official see it?" Do you think student-athletes do not notice the bad sportsmanship exhibited by the coach who rants and raves at an official over a bad call?

It must be continually emphasized to coaches that the opportunity to teach lessons in sportsmanship and ethical behavior does not lie on the playing fields alone. A coach's influence is strong, and the opportunity to teach arises during each and every interaction with student-athletes, beginning with recruitment. Lessons in honesty, sportsmanship, and academic responsibility must be taught daily by action as well as verbally; behavior must be consistent and must demonstrate an uncompromising commitment to sound academic and ethical principles.

Finally, more must be expected from coaches in their role as a visible spokesperson for the university. Although coaches have always served the function of university representative, they have never been expected to promote much more than their own athletic program. Because it is becoming more essential for institutions to communicate their message to the public effectively, this heretofore limited expectation must increase. A coach is often a university's most recognized spokesperson. With visibility comes the responsibility to promote the message to the public that the university is far more about education than athletics. Institutions that do not expect their coaches to understand fully or articulate broadly the themes and accomplishments of the university are wasting a tremendous resource.

In these times of declining public trust and fiscal austerity, each and every component of the community of higher education, including the athletics department, is being challenged to demonstrate how it contributes to the central educational mission of the university in timely and meaningful ways. Coaches, being so highly visible and influential, have a responsibility to provide much-needed educational leadership. For coaches to meet these challenging expectations, however, their job descriptions must be rewritten to include those expectations. At the core of the change in job description is the restoration of the "coach as educator" ideal. Not until coaches, and for that matter administrators, embrace the principle that they are first and foremost educators, and only until they are once again *expected* to be educators, will they and the athletic departments of which they are a part be viewed by the public and academic community as important contributing members of the higher education team.

REVISING COACHING CREDENTIALS

Ironically, virtually no educational standards or criteria exist for becoming a coach; all one needs is a whistle. This situation much change.

According to a 1993 study conducted by the National Association of Athletic Compliance Coordinators' (NAACC) Committee on Athletics and Higher Education, only 49 percent of Division I coaches possess a master's degree, and 2.4 percent do not have even a B.S. or B.A. degree (Gerdy and Estes 1994, 57-70). How can we expect coaches to be positive educational role models when they have not invested in the educational process themselves? Is it not unreasonable to place an individual with a background more suited to sales in a classroom and expect positive teaching results? While it is not always necessary to have a college degree to be an effective teacher, a coach's credibility as an educational role model is linked in part to the extent to which he or she has made a commitment to the educational process. Investing the time, money, and effort to earn an advanced degree demonstrates an individual's belief in and commitment to education.

Coaches insist that they are educators, and as such many believe they should be granted faculty status. The disparity between coaches and faculty in the area of academic preparation, however, is too great for coaches to warrant such a status. In comparing coaches with faculty in the area of degree attainment, 96.8 percent of faculty have earned master's degrees, and 67.4 percent of faculty have doctorates or other terminal (i.e., law, medicine) degrees (*Chronicle of Higher Education* 1994, p. 33). Although, it may be unrealistic to expect all coaches to have doctorates, a master's degree is a reasonable expectation.

If we are going to expect coaches to earn advanced degrees, we must reward them for doing so. For example, incentives can be offered for obtaining an advanced degree while on campus. Is there a single coach's contract that includes a financial bonus to encourage a coach with a B.A. or B.S. to earn a master's degree? Or a coach with a master's to earn a Ph.D.? Placing a greater emphasis on a coach's level of education is a way not only of improving student-athlete welfare, but also of providing more substance to the argument that coaches are teachers and educators.

An example of our lack of commitment to the "coach as educator" model is the way in which graduate assistant coaches are used by athletic departments as legislated by the NCAA. The idea behind the creation of a graduate assistant coaching position was to provide opportunities for young people interested in coaching to further their education while gaining coaching experience. The idea is sound. The implementation of the principle, however, has been badly neglected. Graduate assistant coaches are required to be enrolled in half of a graduate academic load. This standard is reasonable, except that those hours do not have to be in a specific degree program. If the purpose is to provide aspiring coaches an opportunity to further their education, as a minimum, they should be required to take hours toward a specific degree. If we require our student-athletes to be engaged in courses that lead to a specific degree, so too should we apply similar requirements to graduate assistant coaches.

Unfortunately, athletic departments at present are not interested in providing educational opportunity for graduate assistants. They are interested in cheap labor. What is supposed to be a part-time educational opportunity is actually a demanding full-time coaching requirement. Evidence of this desire can be found in the NCAA's replacement of the graduate assistant coaching position with a "restricted-earnings" coach in all sports other than football. The restricted-earnings coach is a full-time position with a salary cap. This position was also hailed as a cost savings initiative. A restricted-earnings coach is limited to receiving $16,000 per year, significantly less money than a standard assistant coach. While it remains permissible to hire a graduate assistant coach in the restricted-earnings slot, most programs will opt to hire a restricted-earnings coach because there is no pretense that it is anything other than a full-time coaching position. Unfortunately, the long-term cost of this seemingly innocuous change in coaching designations is significant because the elimination of the graduate assistant coach will result in fewer coaches with advanced degrees.

Hence, the restricted-earnings position should be eliminated in favor of the graduate assistant position. Schools with no graduate programs could then apply for a waiver to hire a part-time coach. With less than half of Division I coaches holding a master's degree, coaches must be provided educational opportunities and must also be encouraged and supported in their pursuit of those degrees. We need more coaches to invest in the academic process by earning advanced degrees.

If coaches expect others to consider them educators, their level of degree attainment becomes critical. In the academic community, educational attainment is respected and carries great influence. In many regards, educational level is the currency of the higher education community. Whether such an attitude is right or wrong is not the issue. What is important is that athletic departments function within this educational environment. When a group of basketball players travel to another neighborhood or a different playground to play pick-up ball in the summer, different sets of rules apply on different courts. Whatever the number of points required to win the game or regardless of whether the offensive or defensive player is responsible for making a foul call, you play by the rules in effect at that particular court. In the higher education game, degrees are important.

If athletics is to be considered an integral part of the academic community, a greater emphasis has to be placed on the educational backgrounds of coaches during the hiring process. Although academic credentials should not be the only criteria considered during the hiring or evaluation processes, increased weight must be given to their attainment if the "coach as educator" model is to be restored.

PROVIDING PROFESSIONAL DEVELOPMENT OPPORTUNITIES

Once hired, coaches must be provided with meaningful opportunities to refine their teaching skills and to develop more fully as educators. Many professions, including the medical and legal professions, require in-service training on a regular basis. Currently, the professional development opportunities available to coaches fall into two categories. The first are those conducted by coaches associations; as might be expected, the content of such programs has traditionally centered upon strategic or technical aspects of the game itself rather than on the educational issues of coaching. The second opportunity for professional development is offered by the NCAA through conferences or institutions that focus primarily on NCAA rules education.

If the coaching model is to be made legitimate, professional development opportunities must be broadened to incorporate components that relate more closely to the general purposes of the institution, of higher education, and the educational development of student-athletes. Such opportunities should not focus solely on the specific goals of the athletic department. For example, discussion regarding the role of athletics in higher education will challenge coaches to consider that athletics is simply one component of a larger academic community. Presenting issues in student development will raise awareness of the many challenges facing today's college students. Helping coaches use effective retention strategies will facilitate the student-athlete's adjustment to college, thus reducing the likelihood of transfer or withdrawal. Coaches must also be encouraged to consider the educational responsibilities inherent in being a member of an academic community. They must understand that their jobs entail more than simply game strategies and training techniques. An understanding of the history and role of higher education in our society will cause coaches to consider that the academic integrity of the university is not something to be compromised over a 17-year-old recruit.

The programs I have described need to be developed for all coaches, and in particular, new coaches. A coach's first year is critical in shaping his or her attitudes toward student-athletes, educational responsibility, the NCAA, and coaching in general. Never again are coaches likely to be as open to advice about their role as an educator and coach as in that first year. Rookie coaches, however, are not the only coaches who will benefit from participation in professional development programs. With expectations of coaches changing so rapidly, particularly in the area of student-athlete welfare and academic integrity, veteran coaches must have opportunities to remain current. Continuing education forums should be held at conferences and NCAA workshops at conventions and other meetings for coaches. Videotapes could even be developed for national distribution. Because a coach is no longer new on the job does not mean that he or she cannot benefit from continuing education.

A major criticism of coaches is that they have become divorced from the academic process. Those less sympathetic accuse coaches of thinking that they are "above" the educational community. Getting coaches back into a structured educational setting will help them reconnect with the academic process as well as send the message that coaching is far more than planning practice, recruiting, and lining up endorsement deals. Coaches must be challenged to seriously consider the responsibilities inherent in being an educator. And, if athletic departments empower their student-athletes with the suggestions offered in Chapter 5, a new breed of student-athlete, more aware, more informed, and more sophisticated, will emerge. Coaches must have the background and professional development opportunities to meet the challenge of providing academic leadership for this new breed of student-athlete.

Professional development initiatives can also have a positive effect upon universities' efforts to ensure effective institutional control over their athletic departments. The modern-day compliance movement was born at the 1985 Special NCAA Convention. The adoption of the "death penalty" and a provision that allowed the NCAA Committee on Infractions to prohibit coaches who violate rules from coaching at an NCAA institution for up to five years sent a clear message that coaches were expected not only to know the rules but to abide by them. The NCAA followed with significant funding in the form of grants to conferences to develop programs and ensure compliance with rules. The resulting growth in rules-education programs has served to better educate coaches concerning the rules and regulations of the NCAA. Unfortunately, informing coaches of specific rules and threatening severe penalties if they break them is only treating the symptoms of a coach's lack of respect for institutional control and integrity.

Coaches must know specific NCAA rules as well as understand why such rules were adopted. Most important, they need to know why the integrity of the institution, in some cases having been built over a period of 250 years or more, is sacrosanct. When coaches are tempted to break a rule, like any of us, they are more likely to do it if they do not understand it as something more than simply another rule in the NCAA manual. A coach who more fully understands and appreciates the responsibilities inherent in being a representative of an institution will be more likely to do the right thing because it is in the best overall interests of the university.

Many are afraid to challenge powerful coaches to participate. As justification for their own lack of courage, they will perhaps claim that coaches' egos are too big ever to allow them to return to the classroom. The Southeastern Conference, with as many big-name coaches as any conference in the country, requires all coaches new to the league, whether in their first or twenty-fifth year of coaching, to participate in an orientation program that challenges them to think about things other than X's and O's and recruiting. Coaches have responded to this program because it was expected of them, and because that expectation was made clear. Although it may sound like a rigid requirement, a side benefit is that league camaraderie is built when the new coach at Alabama, say, sits next to the new coach at Auburn, both of them hearing the same message for the first time.

INSTITUTIONAL RESPONSIBILITY FOR DEVELOPMENT

Mandatory attendance at these national regional programs is only one component of what must become a comprehensive effort to create a quality system of professional development opportunities. Institutions also bear a major responsibility for the orientation and professional development of their coaches and administrators.

It is not uncommon for a coach to be hired on Monday, arrive on campus on Tuesday to pick up a credit card and recruiting schedule, and hit the road by Tuesday evening. The result is that the individual representing the university to prospective recruits and the general public is someone who has virtually no understanding of or appreciation for the university's programs or culture. Most institutions have faculty orientation and development programs and expectations. Coaches, however, are often exempt from such programs; such exemptions only set the stage for a future of alienation and separation from the academic community.

Many issues are unique to individual campuses. Before a coach represents an institution publicly, he or she should have some understanding of the university's mission, academic policies, personnel, standards of conduct, programs of study, and history. Because coaches are often the most influential and visible representatives of the university, institutions would be well served to develop programs designed to enhance the coach's ability to articulate more effectively the university's mission and to highlight its virtues. Such programs also represent a first step in a more healthy integration of athletic department personnel into the mainstream university community.

Developing a quality institutional orientation program for coaches will also have a positive effect on student-athlete welfare. The foundation for successful adjustment to college, particularly for the student-athlete, is set during the recruitment process when coaches portray the institution in the way they think necessary to convince a prospective student-athlete to sign a National Letter of Intent. It is no surprise that student-athlete discontent often stems from a feeling of having been misled by the coach during recruitment. In many cases, coaches do not knowingly misrepresent what campus life will be like for the student-athlete. More often they are unaware of the institution's culture, programs, or majors. How can coaches accurately represent student life at their institution when they have no appreciation for or understanding of the institution they represent? Therefore, institutions must require their coaches, especially new coaches, to participate in a comprehensive orientation program designed to highlight the institution's culture, history, student life, and student services.

Coaches also interact regularly with high school counselors, principals, and teachers, who, through such interaction, form opinions of the university. These high school administrators influence the college choices of many students (all future "customers" of the university), not just student-athletes. Thus a well-informed coach can benefit not only the athletic department, but university recruitment efforts generally.

The NCAA can play a significant role in helping institutions implement such programs. Legislation should be adopted to require new coaches to participate in an orientation program prior to representing the institution in a recruiting or public relations capacity. My recommendation is that the orientation be a minimum of two days. To take it a step further, evidence of a formal and operational orientation program should be required as part of the NCAA certification program. Coaches and athletic administrators will dismiss this suggestion as simply not workable because the time required to execute it would place the program at a significant recruiting disadvantage. This argument does not hold water. Over time, any institutional disadvantage will balance out as the rule will simply become a part of the process of making a coaching change at all NCAA institutions. An athletic program will not collapse during the 48 hours that new coaches are learning about the institutions they have been hired to represent. Most important, it will send out a clear message that coaching is more than recruiting.

The correlation between the preparation and professional development of coaches and student-athlete welfare is direct. If coaches are often the most influential people in the lives of student-athletes, shouldn't their background, preparation, and development be of utmost importance? Because coaches are often a university's most influential and visible spokespersons, is it not wise to invest in programs that will help coaches better understand and appreciate the institution's mission and goals and enable them to articulate that mission more effectively to the public? Only until a meaningful commitment is made to invest in the professional development of coaches will those coaches be able to fully realize their tremendous potential to contribute to their institution's broader mission. Not until then will the "coach as educator" ideal be resurrected.

REPRIORITIZING COACHES' EVALUATION CRITERIA

The fourth and final element necessary to restore the model of the "coach as educator" involves the criteria upon which coaches are evaluated. Any effort to change the behavior of coaches will be fruitless unless the criteria upon which they are evaluated are altered. For example, where a football coach has been expected to maintain a 10-1 record and receive a major post-season bowl bid every year, the university community may have to adjust those expectations to accept an 8-3 or 7-4 record and a bowl bid, particularly if the coach runs a clean program that produces quality, well-rounded student-athletes who graduate, are positive role models, and contribute to society after their playing days are over.

Coaches should not be forced to decide whether they can afford to take the time necessary to build a program in the right way. If pressured to get the job done quickly, coaches will take gambles. For example, a coach who senses he must turn a program around quickly might feel compelled to recruit a large number of junior college transfers who are academically at risk just so he can win games immediately. The trade-off to this quick fix is that the chances of those junior college transfers graduating are abysmally low. The sounder choice, in terms of building a program the right way, is to recruit academically qualified high school seniors. Of course, that choice entails a trade-off. Results on the court or field are realized more slowly.

Even more troublesome is the way coaches, citing the pressure to win, feel justified in exhibiting types of behavior that simply cannot be tolerated within an educational setting. They compromise the integrity of the institution by cheating in recruiting and engaging in such academically suspect behavior as verbally or physically abusing a student-athlete. They often make excessive fiscal, equipment, or facility demands simply to keep pace with other schools (i.e., an indoor football practice facility in a state with mild weather even though the school's library is having to cut its budget for book acquisitions). Coaches explain away such behavior, regardless of how educationally or fiscally irresponsible it may be, on the basis of "having to win or get fired."

As a result, the presidents of our institutions must understand clearly the relationship between the coach's decision to build a program the right way and the additional time and patience required to build it that way. Moreover, presidents as well as other university leaders must become far more aggressive in articulating to the public, the media, and the alumni this relationship and its effect on the way in which coaches will be evaluated.

If coaches' job descriptions are rewritten in the manner that the presidents, faculty, media, and general public appear to desire, these campus decision makers must then be prepared to support fully their coaches if they do in fact meet these new expectations. If, for example, faculty and presidents decide to reduce the number of special admissions designated for athletics and place a greater emphasis on improving the graduation rates of their student-athletes, they must also be fully committed to standing up to alumni and booster pressure to support the coach who runs a clean program that graduates more student-athletes but posts only a 7-4 or 8-3 record as opposed to a 10-1 record. The price may be heavy, but it is one that presidents, trustees, and other campus leaders must pay if they truly desire reform.

Institutions must create an environment that promotes positive educational and personal development for both student-athletes and coaches. Coaches must be rewarded for striving to become better educators. They must feel confident that when they make decisions that are sound academically but hurt their teams athletically, they will be firmly supported by the entire academic community. A decision to hold a star student-athlete from competition because of poor academic performance must be fully supported, regardless of the outcome of the game. Universities must recognize and support coaches who exhibit sound academic behavior. One small example of how an institution can underscore the importance of the coach's role as an educator is the establishment of a yearly "coach as educator" award. Such an award could be voted upon by student-athletes and could carry with it a significant financial bonus. Faculty are routinely awarded such honors. Why couldn't an athletic department make such a designation? An award like this could be financed by an alumnus or a corporate sponsor interested in linking their product or company with a positive educational initiative.

Only until they feel comfortable that their president will provide the time necessary to build a program the right way will coaches have the freedom to make decisions based upon long-term academic and institutional stability rather than short term, on-the-field results. Only until this relationship is clearly understood will college coaching once again be about teaching and educating rather than winning at any cost. Will coaches still have to win? Of course. Will they still have to win as much or as quickly? Maybe not, provided they meet these off-the-court and field responsibilities more fully and they receive the necessary support from the academic community when they do so.

Coaches hold a big key to true athletic reform. Their actions can greatly damage the integrity and image of an institution. Their attitudes greatly affect student-athlete welfare. Their position as a highly visible representative of the university provides unique imaging opportunities for higher education as it struggles to communicate its story more effectively to the public. But without the necessary background and professional development opportunities, coaches will continue to compromise the integrity of institutions, disregard student-athlete welfare for personal gain, and further damage the image of college athletics and higher education.

Restoration of the "coach as educator" ideal represents a significant challenge in the struggle to justify athletics' place on campus. Unless coaches can demonstrate that they are a valuable part of the higher education community and that what they do is central to the mission of the university, they will continue to be marginalized as high-priced entertainers. If the ideal cannot be resurrected, skepticism regarding the purpose of coaches on the college campus as well as the purpose of the athletic department will continue to grow.

No track coach would ask a long-distance runner to compete as a pole vaulter without adequate training, mentoring, and practice. Similarly, coaches cannot be expected to meet the requirements outlined as part of the New Standard without adequate preparation and nurturing. If we expect coaches to be positive educational role models and conduct their programs with the integrity worthy of their institution and with the long-term academic and personal welfare of their student-athletes as their primary objective, we must create an environment where such behavior is encouraged and valued. Academic achievement, whether it be in a coach's academic credentials, his or her efforts at professional development, or improved graduation rates of student-athletes, must be rewarded. Effectiveness at advancing broad institutional goals must be encouraged and prized. Only until we make a concerted, long-term effort to create an environment that nurtures a coach's commitment to educational responsibility and integrity will the "coach as educator" ideal once again become a reality.

References

Blaney, George. 1993. "Coaches Propose Rule Changes." *Birmingham Post-Herald*. 21 October 1993.

Brickels, Robert "Bo." 1996. Phone conversation with author, September 26.

Eastman and Beaudine. "Broad Range of Talents Required for Today's Athletics Directors." *NCAA News*, 4 November 1994, 1, 13.

Chronicle of Higher Education. 1994. "Characteristics of Full-Time College Professors, 1987." Vol. xli, No. 1. The Almanac Issue.

Galbraith, John Kenneth. 1996. *The Good Society: The Humane Agenda*. New York: Houghton Mifflin.

Gerdy, John, and Lane Estes. "An Assessment of the Educational Levels of NCAA Division I Coaches." *The National Review of Athletics*, January 1994.

Gilley, J. Wade. 1991. *Thinking About American Higher Education: The 1990's and Beyond*. New York: Macmillan/American Council on Education.

Kean, Thomas H. "Time for Action: A New Political Censensus," *Change* 18 (5), (September–October, 1986): 10.

Lester, Robin. 1995. *Stagg's University: The Rise, Decline and Fall of Big-Time Football at Chicago*. Urbana, IL: The University of Illinois Press.

Lipsyte, Robert. 1997. "When 'Kill the Ump' Is No Longer a Joke." *The New York Times*, 19 January, Sec. 8, pp. 1 and 4.

Louis Harris & Associates. 1990. Survey Conducted for The Knight Foundation Commission on Intercollegiate Athletics. Miami, FL.

National Collegiate Athletic Association. 1988. *Studies of Intercollegiate Athletics Report No. 1*. Palo Alto, CA: American Institute for Research.

CHAPTER 7

Athletics—Becoming a Part of the University

Because I assume athletics is an important part of a collegiate education, I believe athletics ought to be subject to the same scrutiny as other parts of the educational institution are.

Bart Giamatti
A Free and Ordered Space

As mentioned in the first chapter, one of the most fundamental challenges facing educational leaders is the job of reversing a decline in public trust in higher education. As has been sufficiently stressed in previous chapters, to think that athletics is not going to be held to the same standard of utility as the English department or medical school at a time when all components of the higher education community are being challenged to streamline operations and justify their worth to the university is presumptuous.

Thus, the most significant issue facing the college athletic community today is not the proliferation of unscrupulous agents, the ever-increasing influx of money and influence from television networks and shoe companies, or the continuing violations of NCAA rules. It is rather the challenge of illustrating how athletics can be more effectively used to assist higher education in fulfilling its mission. While the above-mentioned concerns are all important, they are simply side issues to something far more critical to athletics' survival in the future: the justification of athletics' place within the higher education setting. Such justification will not be easy, nor will it occur overnight. Its worth must be shown over time, not only through athletic department actions but also by the acts and behavior of individuals, particularly those within the athletic department.

For athletics to fulfill its purpose, coaches and athletic administrators must reconsider everything they do, and they must ponder what they will say and how they will say it to make sure they are contributing to the broader goals of the institution. Similarly, faculty and academic leaders need to rethink how athletics' tremendous potential can be better used to further educational goals. The entire higher education community, athletic and academic leaders alike, are responsible for bridging the gap between the athletic and academic communities by reassessing how athletics can be used to contribute more directly to higher education's three-pronged mission of teaching, research, and service. To fulfill the New Standard, we must ensure that athletics is "a part of, rather than apart from," the university.

HELPING TO TELL HIGHER EDUCATION'S STORY

As John Thelin and Lawrence Wiseman pointed out in the quotation at the beginning of Chapter 1, abuses in college sports programs can have a disproportionately negative influence on the public's image of higher education because of the tremendous visibility of sports. The other side of the story, however, is that the same visibility offers higher education a tremendously powerful resource. Athletics is by far the largest and clearest window through which the public views the university. According to an NCAA-sponsored survey, 53 percent of the total American public, 65 percent of men and 43 percent of women, follow college sports (National Collegiate Athletic Association 1991, 22). "Of all the column inches written about the University, I would estimate that 75 percent is regarding the athletic program," Scott Selheimer, director of Sports Information at the University of Delaware, told Bob Torpor in an interview in the March 1995 issue of *Marketing Higher Education* (Torpor 1995, 6).

Thus far, however, that visibility has been used almost exclusively to promote athletics rather than education—college sports is packaged, marketed, and projected purely as entertainment.

To illustrate this point, the National Association of Athletics Compliance Coordinators (NAACC) conducted a study during the 1994-95 academic year in which observers were asked to distinguish the types of educational or athletic themes presented throughout the telecasts of various college basketball and football contests. Sixty-one surveys charted 37 different NCAA basketball contests, and 111 surveys were completed during 42 different football telecasts. At least 58 known individuals charted telecasts. Some respondents were anonymous. The study showed that only 10 percent of those watching a televised college basketball or football contest rated the telecast as "effectively promoting any educational theme," and 1 percent rated the telecast as "very effectively promoting any educational theme." Further, results indicated that only 13 percent of viewers rated the telecast as "effective in informing [the viewer] about the universities, higher education or education generally." Less than one percent (.6 percent) indicated that the telecast was "very effective in informing [the viewer] about the universities, higher education or education generally." And more than half (56 percent) indicated that the telecast charted was "not effective in promoting or highlighting an educational theme" (National Association of Athletics Compliance Coordinators 1995, 4).

Given these results, higher education would be well-served to reevaluate its relationship with television to determine if more effective use can be made of the medium in promoting higher education's goals and mission. All coverage of athletic events, from the content of commercial spots to the subjects discussed during halftime to pregame shows and interviews with coaches, should be evaluated to determine if more effective use can be made of this valuable resource.

It is easy to see how universities have missed these opportunities to use athletics to advance larger institutional purposes. The "management" of athletic programs has always been left to athletic directors and conference commissioners. These individuals simply have not considered control over the content of those broadcasts to be an issue of primary importance. But they cannot be blamed, because university administrators have not fully appreciated the tremendous opportunity televised games provide to effectively promote the value, mission, and goals of higher education. Corporate America has recognized the power of television to send messages and project images to the public. That is why advertising agencies are paid millions of dollars to develop strategies for selling their clients' products or services. Higher education should seize the same opportunity to communicate its message and shape its image through telecasts of its athletic contests.

The issue of the best use of telecasts did not escape the scrutiny of the 1991 report of The Knight Foundation Commission on Intercollegiate Athletics. "Presidents should control their institution's involvement with commercial television," the report specified. "It is time that institutions clearly prescribe the policies, terms and conditions of the televising of athletics events" (Knight Foundation 1991, 14).

Television executives, however, will claim that educational imaging is not what the public wants. Athletic department representatives will assert that the public is only interested in the game itself, citing the fact that a university-sponsored chemistry lecture has yet to draw 50,000 paying fans and a national television audience. While that may be true, how do we know that the viewing public would not be interested in a creative linkage of the institution's athletic program to the other programs it offers? Corporate advertising campaigns often link a highly visible and popular product to other company products that are less well known. For example, various snack foods owned by Pepsico are shown or referred to during ads featuring Pepsi.

NBC's presentation of the 1996 Olympic Games offers an example of why claims that the viewing audience is interested only in the actual sporting event are unfounded. While receiving criticism in some quarters (mostly from the media) for featuring a large number of human interest stories and historical segments (such as a 12-minute account of Atlanta's role in the Civil War), the average household rating for these Olympics was up 26 percent from the ratings for the 1992 Barcelona Games (NBC Sports, 1996). The bottom did not drop out of the ratings when stories or images other than those directly related to the actual sporting event were presented. NBC successfully used the Olympics to paint a larger picture—to tell a broader story—a story that had more to do with history and the lives of the athletes than with their athletic achievements.

There is also a high degree of arrogance implied in the claim that those who follow sports have such narrow interest as to be incapable of appreciating educational themes. Demographic research indicates otherwise. According to a 1995 New York Times readership study, 81 percent of the weekday readers of the New York Times sports section are college graduates. And the median annual household family income of those weekday readers is $78,300.

Further, a significant percentage of college sports viewers are interested in higher education as evidenced by the fact that they have already invested in the product itself. A 1991 study conducted for the NCAA by Louis Harris & Associates showed a strong relationship between education level and the number of college athletic events watched on television. Viewers with only a high school degree watched, on average, significantly fewer (15) college sports events per year than did viewers who attended college some period of time (21), graduated from college (23), or did postgraduate work (22). This study also revealed a strong relationship between level of income and the number of college sports events watched on television. Viewers with an income of $25,000 or less watched, on average, 14 college sports events per year. This was in comparison to 20 sports events watched per year for viewers with an annual income of from $25,001 to $50,000, 25 times per year for viewers with an income of $50,001 to

$75,000, and 24 times per year for viewers with an income of more than $75,000 (National Collegiate Athletic Association 1991, 27). According to a 1987 College Football Association study, 47 percent of the viewers of televised CFA games either attended (22 percent) or graduated (25 percent) from college. Further, more than half (51 percent) of households viewing CFA contests had children below the age of 17, all potential consumers of higher education (College Football Association 1987).

When these key demographic elements are combined, as can be done through Neilson's television rating system, the results are even more revealing. For example, during the 1996 NCAA men's basketball tournament on CBS, viewership was 20 percent to 50 percent greater among homes with yearly household incomes of at least $40,000 with children under the age of 18, compared to the average household viewing those contests. The same holds true for homes with yearly household incomes of at least $40,000 where the head of the household has at least one year of college education (Zenith Media Services, Inc., 1997).

To categorically claim that such viewers would not be interested in educational themes woven through a televised athletic event is not a proven statistic. To dismiss the opportunity to image education in exciting and creative ways to such a large number of either former or potential students and their parents is simply shortsighted. And could it be that such figures warrant reconsideration of the valuable exposure that a televised college sports event offers as it relates to university fund raising and public influence?

A NEW KIND OF TV CONTRACT

To use television to promote higher education more effectively, we must reconsider the terms and stipulations of the television contracts we sign to broadcast our sporting events. Let's take, for example, the NCAA's current seven-year, $1.7 billion television contract with CBS for the rights to televise its men's basketball tournament. The tremendous sum of $1.7 billion has been well spent. Besides supporting a major portion of the NCAA's national office operating budget, the revenue has been used for grants to enhance tutoring and other academic support services for student-athletes. It has also been used to develop education programs for coaches and initiatives to improve institutional control over athletic department operations. It has been used to create a fund to aid needy student-athletes, to finance catastrophic injury insurance for all NCAA institutions, and to create a reserve fund to guard against a future drop in television revenue.

Obviously, this contract was good for college sports. But was it as good as it could have been for higher education? Could it be that in the attempt to maximize financial return, higher education has given away too much control over its "product" and hence the way in which it is portrayed and imaged? What if, for example, the NCAA had negotiated a package with CBS that called for less cash, say $1.5 billion, but provided for increased cooperation by the network in helping to use athletics and television to tell the positive story of higher education?

One possibility would be to increase the number and quality of promotional spots for institutions. We're all familiar with the brief spots that are broadcast during NCAA games. They feature quick tours of attractive campuses, with a few shots of laboratories and rapid-fire narration of statistics on enrollment, degrees offered, and honors won by faculty and graduates. Sandwiched between more technically sophisticated commercials for automobiles and soft drinks, the staid university spots showing chemistry students huddled around a Bunsen burner or coeds walking across campus do not measure up as exciting "imaging." But negotiating more 30-second spots for higher-quality university promos is one small component of what should be a broad-based initiative to use the tremendous imaging opportunities provided by televised college sports.

Perhaps higher education leaders could also negotiate for increased influence in the selection and training of game announcers to ensure that they have some understanding of the goals and mission of higher education, and not solely the dynamics of the forward pass or jump shot. During timeouts, why couldn't announcers be provided information that would enable them to interject a sound bite promoting an educational program or an accomplishment of one of the universities involved in the contest rather than a meaningless statistic about a long-forgotten guard on the 1923 championship team?

"Player of the Game" features should be eliminated in favor of segments that highlight student-athletes' accomplishments off the field. During timeouts, why couldn't administrators of the institutions involved provide information on their admissions and financial-aid processes to encourage potential students and their parents to consider the college opportunities available? Providing more information on the process of applying to a college and on the value of attending it is becoming increasingly important as most high schools are woefully understaffed in the area of guidance counseling. The NCAA has taken a step in this direction with its effort to inform prospective student-athletes of NCAA initial eligibility standards through 30-second infomercials. But this well-intentioned effort simply exemplifies the limited way in which television exposure has been used, for the sports target only prospective student-athletes and not prospective students generally. Informing prospective student-athletes of NCAA eligibility standards is important, but informing all prospective students of admissions processes and financial-aid opportunities will have a far broader and longer-lasting impact on higher education.

Higher education must become more adept at using athletics to communicate its message. For example, one subject might be Louisiana State University's Business and Technology Center, an incubator for new and start-up businesses, and how it is helping to launch or provide management assistance to hundreds of new businesses. Another example might be how the cancer research being conducted at the University of Alabama at Birmingham may one day save the life of a viewer's child. Another subject might be how one of the student-athlete's hopes is to become a doctor and to save lives of cancer patients. This would be a cause as worthy of celebration as a teammate's efforts to reach the pros. Another idea might be that the correlation between higher education and future income is dramatic. Televised games present an opportunity for higher education to illustrate specifically how it contributes to improving the lives of individual citizens and to let people know that higher education is a resource available to all.

Ira Berkow, in a 30 March 1992 column in the *New York Times,* articulated the need for such a change in approach when he observed.

> Once in a while we read a visual on the screen that informs us that the young man at the free throw line is majoring in something or other. But that's the end of it. Take us into some of their classrooms. Most important: Make it honest. From the heart. The real deal. Why shouldn't a student-athlete talk about the joys of learning? . . . What if, say, the flying forward for Indiana discussed an American history course he's taking, and how the background for the start of the Civil War has clarified something for him? . . . Or another player talked about a speech class, from which he learned that the language of the marketplace is not the language of the streets? (Berkow 1992)

Television needs college athletics every bit as much as college athletics needs television. Networks must fill program time. Network executives know that college sports sell. Televised college athletics is a hot property. The public wants to see sports and will continue to watch them even if more time is carved out of broadcasts to promote educational themes. While the bright lights and cheering crowds of athletics are easier to package as an exciting "product," more time and money should be spent developing creative ways to advertise education. Creative and captivating sound bites, infomercials, and images about higher education might hold the attention of viewers otherwise inclined to "channel surf" or leave their sets to get a snack. If one network did not appreciate higher education's need to project its successes more effectively, other networks might.

Televised games, as higher education's most visible activity, can be used to further the general goals of universities rather than the specific goals of athletic programs. The issue of control over the way in which higher education is presented and promoted must be placed squarely on the table when contracts are negotiated. The number of games, commercials, and dollar amounts are negotiated during contract talks; the way higher education is imaged and marketed during sports broadcasts should be negotiated as well. Television executives will balk at attempts to influence the way in which games are presented, indicating that such efforts will infringe upon their duty to report the often controversial realities of big-time athletics. But the purpose here is not to cover up problems when they arise. If there are negatives to report, networks have an obligation to report them. Rather, the purpose of such efforts is to place more emphasis on presenting the game within a much broader educational framework than is currently the case.

To begin to work toward that goal, the individuals directly responsible for and involved with the negotiation of television and radio contracts must change. Athletic directors and conference commissioners cannot be the only institutional representatives conducting such negotiations because their primary purpose, understandably, will always be to promote more athletics. While reducing athletic departments' autonomy over the negotiation of television rights will be a tough sell for college administrators, it is certainly worth the effort.

The place to start is to communicate to athletic administrators that a university is an educational institution. Although some would disagree, a coach is never bigger than the athletic program, and the program is never bigger than the university. Athletics is simply one of many tools the institution has at its disposal to further its educational priorities. Although athletic administrators may resist giving up a degree of control over the way "their" product is presented, the fact is that college athletics is not "their" product. It belongs to higher education. Thus, representatives from institutional advancement offices rather than athletic department personnel should have ultimate responsibility for negotiating both institutional and conference contracts.

Demonstrating that sports make a positive contribution to higher education is particularly important in the wake of the recurrent recruiting violations and other scandals that have made many citizens cynical about the ethics and value of college sports. The image and credibility of sports will continue to decline as the public tires of the hypocrisy of our claim that college athletics is about education when the message we broadcast is entirely about money and winning. Weaving educational messages that promote the broader substance of education throughout telecasts of sporting events will not only be of value to higher education generally, but can help athletic programs shore up their own image both with the public and within the higher education community.

If the messages delivered through televised athletic contests are more balanced, athletics can help higher education regain public trust. If over time our actions reflect positive educational values, the public will once again come to view an investment in our colleges and universities as a wise one. Some people may question whether the prospective benefits of using contract money to "sell" higher education during televised games will offset the short-term loss of revenue. The shift, however, is a long-term investment. A television contract is not simply a matter of dollars. There is value in creating a more positive institutional image or in informing potential customers of the quality and benefit of your product. Television has a powerful influence on the public, specifically the people who vote on tax referenda for education, who influence politicians, and who attend our schools and send their children to them. Until higher education views the telecasts of college athletic events as an opportunity to interface with that public in an educational rather than simply an athletic context, any television contracts that the NCAA, conferences, or institutions sign will result in a lost opportunity to promote higher education to its fullest.

Further institutions of higher education, particularly large state universities, define to some degree the image of the state itself. A conference, for example, can serve to project an image for an entire region of the country. The Southeastern Conference is comprised of the major state universities from the nine states that make up the bulk of the Southeast. The image that is projected during a telecast of an SEC football game will for many people define not only those SEC schools, but an entire region. Is this area of the country best served by projecting a one-dimensional, athletically focused image? Displaying an increased sensitivity to the broader state or region can contribute to higher education's purpose of serving the needs of a state or region.

Athletic events are also broadcast on radio networks and covered in local and national newspapers and magazines. Athletic departments produce an incredible amount of material promoting their teams—media guides, game programs, and posters. Athletic events themselves offer an opportunity to address a captive audience on campus. But once again, the messages and themes associated with these publications and events are almost exclusively sports related. Thus, every point at which the athletic department interfaces with the public should be identified and evaluated to determine if that opportunity can be used to promote general university themes more effectively.

RESTRUCTURING ATHLETIC DEPARTMENTS

A major step in moving toward broader exposure of the university through athletics is to remove the sports information and marketing departments from under direct athletic department control. One of the primary justifications for incorporating athletics into higher education was that its visibility could be used to promote the virtues of the school to a wider audience. It is arguable, however, whether athletic departments have done an effective job of promoting educational themes. Moving the authority for the promotional arms of the athletic department to the university's office of institutional advancement would better serve the interests of the institution and begin to restore the proper relationship between athletics and higher education.

For example, rather than interviewing a sports personality during half-time of a radio broadcast, why not allow a faculty member to tell about the findings of a recently completed research project? Or couldn't the traditional action shot on the program cover at a ballgame be replaced by artwork created by a student? Although the promotional materials produced and activities conducted will not change overnight, as a result of being more directly exposed to institutional influences and being held accountable to the office of institutional advancement, instutional messages and themes will be woven into athletic promotions over time.

Further, moving this athletic department function to the office of institutional advancement will provide the institution more authority to work with coaches to reemphasize their role and improve their effectiveness as a spokesperson for the university. Coaches are asked to speak to literally hundreds of alumni clubs, civic organizations, and youth groups and are interviewed on radio and television on a regular basis. Once again, the message communicated is often exclusively athletic. If coaches are provided with information regarding institutional messages, programs of the school, and the school's accomplishments, they can incorporate this information into their speeches.

An example of a lost opportunity for a coach to speak on behalf of his university helps to illustrate the importance of the concept more clearly even than positive examples. During a nationally televised interview, a high-profile coach was asked to comment on the firing of a colleague. After the coach expressed his own dismay, the show's host responded, "Well, after all, college athletics is nothing more than a business, isn't it?" The coach's loss for a response was a lost opportunity for his employer. His silence was damning in that it reinforced the general perception that athletics is really not part of the educational function of a university.

A coach who had been trained to think about his or her role in the promotion of the educational function of the institution could have responded with intelligence to this negative allegation and would have been prepared to correct misconceptions whenever necessary. This coach could have made the point that although there may be some business principles that apply to intercollegiate athletics, the main function is to provide an educational experience for thousands of young people. Worse, this coach had an opportunity to address a national television audience; nowhere in his 20-minute interview did he even attempt to weave any educational or institutional messages or themes into his responses.

The intended purpose of this book is not to turn a college football game into a National Geographic special; however, with the proper preparation, a little creativity, and the necessary commitment, educational themes can be comfortably woven into the course of the dialogue. Institutions can no longer afford to squander such opportunities. Being an effective advocate for education in general, and higher education in particular, must become a fundamental component of a coach's job description.

A similar case can be made for incorporating the athletic fund-raising operation into the university's office of institutional advancement. A primary justification for formally incorporating athletics into higher education was that it would contribute to the institution's efforts to raise the resources necessary for survival. Those resources took the form of money from alumni and the corporate community, as well as political favor from state legislators. Nevertheless, those expectations have been largely unmet due to the isolation of the athletic department from the mainstream campus community.

While athletic events provide an excellent backdrop against which the institution can entertain potential donors, and highly visible coaches and athletic directors can assist institutional fund-raising efforts by making speeches and public appearances, most athletic department fundraising efforts are directed at raising money specifically for the athletic program. Even in cases where athletics is involved in the university's general fund-raising efforts, the nature of the event often suggests that the coach is "on loan" to the university or that the athletic department is doing the university "a favor." This attitude exists because at most institutions, the athletic fundraising operation is independent from the institution's fund-raising operation. No one is doing anyone "a favor." Raising money for the institution is the responsibility of every staff member. This is particularly true in the case of athletic department personnel, inasmuch as resource acquisition is used as one of athletics' primary justifications for being on campus.

Integrating the athletic department marketing and fund-raising operations into the university's office of institutional advancement does not mean that efforts to promote or raise money for the athletic department would be discontinued. Rather, those efforts would continue as part of university-wide efforts to generate publicity and resources. If a fundamental justification for athletics is that it generates exposure and resources for the university, then all efforts related to these functions should be subject to the direct oversight and control of the university's office of institutional advancement. Despite the claim from athletic department officials that they work closely with the university's office of institutional advancement, such cooperation is superficial, considering the separation and mistrust that exists between most athletic departments and the rest of the academic community. This situation must improve significantly if higher education is to fully tap athletics' potential to contribute to the mission of universities. Universities must insist that athletic departments become better team players in matters relating to institutional advancement.

COLLEGE ATHLETICS AND COMMUNITY SERVICE

Former Harvard University President Derek Bok, in his provocative work *Universities and the Future of America*, argues that our ability to address effectively the array of social issues we face ultimately depends on the values of individual citizens. Bok poses the following question:

> Since values are so decisive, are our universities doing enough to build in our society—especially among its most influential members and leaders—a strong sense of civic responsibility, ethical awareness and concern for the interests of others?
>
> [Although universities] may not have any special capacity to prescribe solutions for the nation's ills, they are better equipped than any other institution to produce the knowledge needed to arrive at effective solutions and to prepare the highly educated people required to carry them out. (Bok 1990, 7, 11)

Bok is talking about community service—its value and the responsibility we have as educators to promote it.

As discussed in Chapter 2, service is one of the three vehicles through which higher education meets societal needs. With many in the media, general public, and academe challenging athletics to justify its place on campus, a more organized and aggressive effort to promote community service through our highly visible athletic departments might be a way to counter some of this criticism. While most athletic programs and their student-athletes are involved in community service, the degree of involvement varies greatly, often hinging upon the interests of a particular coach or student-athlete. To make such involvement consistent, ongoing, and substantial, a formal commitment to community service must become a significant component of all athletic departments' mission statements.

Many in college athletics will react to this proposal by asking, "Do you mean to tell me that we should not only be responsible for recruiting better prepared student-athletes, educating and graduating them, keeping them out of trouble, winning games and generating money, but we're also responsible for alleviating hunger, curing cancer, housing the homeless, wiping out illiteracy, eradicating drug abuse and teenage pregnancy, and stopping youngsters from dropping out of school?"

Of course an athletic department cannot change the world. But there are ways in which it can make a more significant contribution to helping higher education achieve its service-related goals. As members of the education community, student-athletes and coaches are in a unique position to become more actively involved in education-related issues such as illiteracy and school dropouts. As one of the most visible enterprises in our society, college athletics is particularly well equipped to address issues like drug abuse, teenage pregnancy, racial prejudice, and gender equality. Community service offers an excellent opportunity to team up with the general university community, not only to contribute to greater public good, but also to become more integrated into the academic community.

Such an initiative by an athletic department would be met with great approval from the academic community. Many colleges and universities have stepped up their efforts to teach students lessons in social responsibility. Universities are developing more courses that allow students to combine classroom learning with service projects. Again, the inconsistent nature of athletic departments' commitment to the ideal of teaching students social responsibility is not a result of a lack of ability or sensitivity, but rather a product of a system that defines athletic department success only in terms of wins and losses and revenue generated. If given the proper attention and commitment, athletic departments will be able to develop creative and exciting ways to supplement broader university goals in this area.

As an example of how this works, an athletic department could work with the institution's alumni office to conduct an outreach program at the site of a road contest for each of its teams. Such an initiative could work as follows. Suppose Duke University's women's basketball team was scheduled to play a game against Georgia Tech in Atlanta. Duke's alumni office could ask the local alumni club in Atlanta to organize an outreach event, whether it be a visit to a hospital or conducting a clinic for disadvantaged youth, that would feature the student-athletes. Not only would this event be worthwhile and educational for the student-athletes, it would provide an opportunity to network with successful alumni. Duke would also garner positive public exposure in the Atlanta area, and the alumni would be involved in a "feel good" activity sponsored by their alma mater. Who knows, the next time the school approaches them for a donation, they might be more inclined to give one. Or if they already have made a donation, to give even more! Student-athletes enjoy a meaningful experience while making alumni contacts; the athletic department gets to demonstrate that it can contribute to the mission of the university in a new and exciting way; and the college might raise some extra money. Everyone wins! With commitment and creative thinking, athletics can be used to bring the college community together in more ways than simply providing a place to watch a game. Service and outreach provide an excellent vehicle to accomplish this task.

Athletic departments must also become more involved in K-12 education. A recurring theme in the dialogue regarding higher education reform is that colleges and universities must become more actively involved in education at all levels—from kindergarten through high school. A 1993 report on higher education by a group of 16 leading educators, business leaders, and foundation executives titled *An American Imperative: Higher Expectations for Higher Education* concluded that "colleges and universities need to understand that their business is all of education—learning. They can no longer afford to concern themselves exclusively with *higher* education" (Wingspread, 1993, p.19).

"Society needs and American higher education must provide a front and center engagement with the issues of elementary and secondary education—the issue of the public schools in our society," echoes C. Peter McGrath, president of the National Association of State Universities and Land Grant Colleges (Wingspread 1993, p.111).

Athletics can be a major contributor to higher education's efforts to increase its involvement in K-12 education. Again, what better campus group to reach out to young people than our highly visible student-athletes and coaches? College athletic programs, as part of their increased commitment to community service, have an opportunity to become more directly involved with higher education's efforts to reconnect with K-12 education.

There are many examples of athletic departments reaching out to elementary and secondary schools. The University of Georgia athletic department has joined in a partnership with the Clarke County Board of Education and adopted a local school. Athletic department staff and student-athletes provide assistance to a local elementary school in a variety of ways, including serving as mentors, classroom readers, and volunteers for special events. The University of Maryland has taken outreach efforts to a new level with its Team Maryland program. This program combines academic work with community service. Student-athletes take a semester-long class on leadership and earn academic credit for such activities. Prior to disbanding, the College Football Association had initiated a particularly creative way to partner with the corporate community in reconnecting with K-12 education. It organized the CFA/Hitachi Promise of Tomorrow Scholarship Program. This innovative program offered a $5,000 scholarship to each of the 67 CFA member institutions for a senior or graduate student who intended to continue academic work in an undergraduate or postgraduate program that was designed to pursue a career in education.

Like it or not, college athletics is the most visible component of higher education. Rather than bemoan the fact, we can recognize and accept it, not as a burden, but as an opportunity to use visibility to strengthen athletics' place on campus. Student-athletes and coaches can have an enormous impact on people, particularly children. Athletic departments can provide the community more than simply a place to watch a basketball game on Saturday night. They can make a difference, particularly in advancing the message that education is important, staying in school is important, and reading is important.

Such an ambitious community service effort will raise the issue of excessive time demands being placed upon student-athletes. "Student-athletes have a very full schedule," argues the coach. "When are they going to find the time to study with such community service obligations to fill? Anyway, we can not force them to do it." Again, this is an instance of selling our student-athletes short. If we can require student-athletes to attend study hall, alumni functions, and "voluntary" workouts, we can require involvement in community service. While their schedules are full, the same coach would have no trouble demanding an extra hour or two per week for an individual workout, weight training, or a film session.

If we consider what is in the best long-term educational and personal development interests of our student-athletes, we can see the advantage of requiring an hour or two per week or every other week devoted to community service, for it will have far more lasting and meaningful impact than spending that time in the weight room. Community service not only teaches lessons in empathy, civic involvement, and personal responsibility, it also significantly contributes to a student-athlete's experiencing of a well-balanced college life. Student social involvement of this nature should be regular and fully supported and facilitated by the athletic department, preferably as part of broader university efforts to encourage student service. Serious consideration should be given to requiring a specific number of hours of community service as part of the institutional scholarship agreement. Some institutions have required community service of students at one time or another, most notably, the University of Minnesota and the University of Southern California.

An aggressive community service component incorporated into all athletic department mission statements would be another way in which athletics could show itself a valuable contributor to the higher education team. And while it may not have much of an effect on the playing field, it greatly contributes to the success of the athletic department as measured by the New Standard.

OPPORTUNITY, DIVERSITY, AND GENDER EQUITY

The importance of addressing the issue of diversity on our athletic department staffs is obvious, especially as it relates to the welfare and retention of minority student-athletes. Tinto writes, "While role modeling seems to be effective in retention programs generally, it appears to be especially important among those programs concerned with disadvantaged students of color. For them, more so than the 'typical' college student, the availability of like-person role models who have successfully navigated the waters of majority institutions appears to be an especially important component to their own success on campus" (Tinto 1993, 186). But the significance of this issue goes beyond student-athlete welfare.

"We would love to hire a minority, but qualified minorities and women are hard to find." How often this excuse has been used when discussing candidates to fill administrative or coaching vacancies in intercollegiate athletics? Why, with such a large pool of minority student-athletes in our programs as participants, has it been so difficult to find "qualified" candidates who are interested in pursuing a career in college athletics? Why is the well apparently so dry? The answer: Because you reap what you sow.

As has been well documented, our society is becoming increasingly diverse. According to the Hudson Institute's report *Workforce 2000*, women will make up 47 percent and nonwhites 29 percent of the workforce by the year 2000 (Hudson Institute 1987). Such an increasingly multicultural population presents tremendous challenges. Higher education will be asked to provide leadership in addressing the challenges presented by diversity, and as its most visible activity, athletics will be expected to play a major role in contributing to higher education's efforts to meet these multicultural challenges. It is especially important, therefore, that issues of gender equity and minority opportunity be addressed by the athletic community in an aggressive and responsible manner.

Some might argue that athletics is not in a position to provide leadership on this issue given the small percentage of minorities and women in athletic

department decision-making positions. For example, in 1996 only 19 percent of NCAA women's athletic programs were directed by a female head
administrator. That number dropped to 9 percent for Division I institutions. And 48 percent of the coaches of NCAA women's teams were
women, which mirrors the percentage in Division I (Acosta and Carpenter
1996). According to the NCAA Minority Opportunities and Interests
Committee's four-year study of race demographics of member institutions
(excluding the historically black colleges and universities), in 1993-94, less
than 4 percent of NCAA directors of athletics and only 7 percent of
NCAA head coaches were black. In the revenue-producing sports of
football and basketball, less than 8 percent of head coaches were black, and
that number rose to only 10 percent in Division I (National Collegiate
Athletic Association 1994).

These shortfalls are particularly damning considering the previously
mentioned high percentage of minority student-athletes participating in
athletics, especially in the revenue-generating sports of basketball and
football. According to the 1996 NCAA Division I Graduation Rate Report,
24 percent of scholarship student-athletes entering Division I athletics
programs from 1986 to 1989 were African Americans. The numbers are
particularly high in football (44 percent), men's basketball (59 percent),
and women's basketball (34 percent) (National Collegiate Athletic Association 1996, 622).

Despite these disparities, athletics provides a significant number of
educational opportunities, most notably in the case of black students and
more so than any other program in higher education. While the numbers of
minorities and women in decision-making positions remain disappointingly
low, athletics continues to be uniquely positioned to call attention to these
issues. Thus, aggressively addressing the issue of identifying and hiring
qualified women and minorities for positions of authority in college athletic
programs is crucial. But how do we accomplish the task?

Building the ranks of minorities and women in athletic-department
decision-making positions will not be easy, nor will it occur overnight.
Some progress can be expected as our population becomes more diversified. As white male decision makers retire, positions should be filled by
more minorities and women. So, a degree of progress in this area seems
likely. Following the 1996 football season, however, 23 Division I-A head
football coaching positions became available. Yet only one was filled with
an African-American (New Mexico State). For that reason, we should not
leave an issue of such importance to evolve on its own; rather, we need to
search for ways to facilitate the integration of these underrepresented
groups into the college athletic establishment. We must commit to the

development of both short- and long-term, comprehensive strategies to address these shortfalls.

Let me make some suggestions. The college athletic community, both collectively and within individual institutions, needs to make a firm commitment to improving minority representation at all levels. A commitment to diversifying the ranks of college coaches and administrators must become a part of our organizational mind-set. Pressure for a more diverse intercollegiate athletic community will not go away. If progress is not steady and meaningful, our exposure to criticism will continue to increase. It appears that NCAA institutions are committing themselves to addressing this issue, but as evidenced in the previously mentioned Division I-A situation, we have not come as far as we need to. It is clearly a subject that is on all our agendas, however, largely due to pressure from the media, Congress, and from the Black Coaches Association (BCA).

In the short term, athletic leaders are in a position to identify and recruit individuals who may not have the "traditional" job experience of white male candidates. But these candidates have other qualifications that make it to our advantage to diversify and imperative that they be represented in our educational systems. We must stop wasting time and energy making excuses for not hiring minorities and women and find ways to get the job done. There are ways to help bring about change in this area. One example is that when hiring a business manager or marketing director, rather than hiring from within our own athletic departments, we can broaden the applicant pool of qualified minorities and women by tapping the resources of our business and marketing trade associations.

But simply hiring more women and minorities is not enough. Once hired, this new workplace diversity must be effectively managed to foster an environment where minorities and women can achieve success. Just as minority student-athletes face particular challenges on an overwhelmingly white campus, minority and women coaches and administrators have needs that are unique in an environment that is dominated by white males. In an attempt to highlight the importance of managing diversity, the Southeastern Conference committed the time and resources in 1993 to conduct a diversity training workshop at each of its institutions. The purpose of these workshops was to assist coaches and administrators in creating multicultural, nonbiased learning environments in which all student-athletes, coaches, and administrators can succeed. While a one-day diversity workshop simply represents a small step in addressing diversity issues, it is a start. These programs can serve to place diversity issues on the table for all to acknowledge and address. The NCAA is currently developing similar programs for all its member institutions.

A long-term strategy to promote diversity in the college athletic community needs to be developed, and it begins with the student-athlete experience itself. Current minority and women student-athletes are among the coaches, athletic directors, conference commissioners, and officials of the future. Or so it should be. If minority and women student-athletes have a quality intercollegiate athletic experience, an experience where they believe that they were provided a legitimate opportunity to earn a well-balanced academic, social, and athletic experience, they will be more inclined to invest in a career in intercollegiate athletics. If, for example, more minority student-athletes graduate, the pool of those individuals able to consider a career in college athletics will expand. With only 37 percent of minority student-athletes for the entering classes of 1983-84 through 1986-87 graduating, the pool of qualified minority student-athletes starts out small. Thus, the starting point is a recommitment to the principle that the primary purpose of college athletics is for all student-athletes to earn a degree and have a well-balanced academic, social, and athletic experience. The quality of the student-athlete experience can have a direct impact on the future pool of qualified athletic administrators, coaches, and officials.

For women, the issue is a bit different. Women student-athletes are graduating in high numbers (66 percent). However, there are far fewer women than men student-athletes receiving athletic scholarships. According to the 1996 Graduation Rate Report, only 33 percent of all athletic scholarships are awarded to female student-athletes (National Collegiate Athletic Association 1996, 622). So while it appears that the women who participate in intercollegiate athletics are taking full advantage of the educational opportunity afforded through a scholarship, the initial pool of women student-athletes from which to draw is decidedly smaller than the pool of men. Thus, it is no surprise when a 200-member applicant pool for an assistant athletic director position contains only five women applicants.

Institutional and conference student-athlete committees can play an important role in developing the coaches and administrators of the future. Involvement in such committees exposes student-athletes to the issues of the day and allows them to envision themselves in a career in intercollegiate athletics. During a 1994 meeting of the Southeastern Conference Student-Athlete Advisory Committee, two student-athletes, one male and one female and both minorities, indicated their interest in becoming an intern at the conference office. That was a long way from three years earlier when we had to go out and recruit a minority candidate to fill the same position.

Maybe it was because they could envision themselves in that position after meeting and working with the conference's intern at the time, who was an African American. Or maybe it was because, as a member of our student-athlete committee, they discovered that there is more to running an athletic program than pumping up the balls and rolling them out on the floor. Could it have been that such exposure convinced them that a career in college athletics would be interesting and challenging? Creating viable, working student-athlete committees can have more far-reaching benefits than simply giving student-athletes a voice. Such committees not only provide a vehicle to improve student-athlete welfare, they also represent the front end of an identification, nurturing, and mentoring system for enlarging the pool of potential future minority and women athletic administrators, coaches, and officials.

It is to our advantage to mentor and track student-athletes who show promise for a career in intercollegiate athletics. Such candidates require leadership and graduate school opportunities after their playing days are over. Although progress has been made in creating new internship and postgraduate scholarship opportunities at all levels, these opportunities must be expanded.

The task will take commitment as well as the development and implementation of both short- and long-term strategies. Once established, however, the progress will be self-perpetuating. A better student-athlete experience for minorities and women means more minorities and women interested in, and qualified for, positions as coaches and administrators, which means more minority and women role models for minority and women student-athletes, and, ultimately, a better student-athlete experience for minorities and women. The circle will become whole. It can be done. It will, however, require commitment, and it starts with the student-athlete experience.

ATHLETICS AS A LINE ITEM IN THE INSTITUTIONAL BUDGET

Nothing would do more to facilitate the integration of the athletic department into the university community than to include the department as a line item in the university's budget. This idea was floated by Dick Schultz, then executive director of the NCAA, in his 1991 "State of the Association Address." Regrettably, it received little serious consideration.

At many Division I institutions, athletics is a stand-alone enterprise, separate from the university in all matters financial. In some cases, state statutes actually prohibit universities from supplementing athletic department budgets with general university funds. At others, university policy requires athletics to be financially self-supporting. Obviously, without a university financial safety net, there is tremendous pressure on athletic department officials to generate money to fund a broad-based program for both men and women.

Direct university governance over athletic department budgets will have many benefits. Overseeing budgets in this way will bring a higher level of fiscal control and will allow closer institutional examination of athletic department programs and objectives. The clear message is that athletics has important enough educational value for it to be fully incorporated into the financial workings of the institution. It will enable the university to determine exactly how much of an investment it wishes to make in athletics. Finally, it will contribute significantly to a healthier integration of athletics into the mainstream university community.

In his address, Schultz articulated this point as follows:

> Athletic departments should be funded like any other university department or auxiliary enterprise. A budget should be submitted and approved, and all staff compensation should come through normal university channels. Athletic departments should develop as much revenue as possible by institutionally approved methods, and any shortfalls should be covered by the university and any profits should go to the general fund. Only then can athletics hold its proper place on campus. (Schultz 1991)

Schultz's comments were quickly dismissed as unworkable or unrealistic; athletic directors are hesitant to surrender control over "their" department's fiscal affairs. But as in the case of athletic department visibility and exposure, the resources spent and generated by athletics are not "their" resources but rather university resources to be generated and spent for the benefit of the whole university. In states where such an arrangement is prohibited, higher education leaders can begin to lobby state legislators to make the necessary changes to permit it.

Incorporating the athletic department as a line item in the general institutional budget is not only an achievable goal, as evidenced by the fact that at many institutions such an arrangement already exists, it is imperative if athletic departments are to realize their capacity to contribute to their institution's mission and become "a part of rather than apart from" the institution. Such change will fundamentally alter the institution's perception of its return-on-investment in athletics. The result, as suggested in Chapter 1, will be a greater institutional ROI in athletics as measured by the New Standard.

BEING A RESPONSIBLE TEAM MEMBER

The purpose of this chapter has been to identify specific ways in which athletics can contribute more directly to higher education's mission. Rethinking the way in which its high visibility, particularly its television exposure, can be used to promote the broader goals of the institution is perhaps athletics' most powerful and influential attribute. If effectively harnessed, the benefit to higher education can be enormous. Incorporating an aggressive community service commitment into athletic department mission statements can result in a solid, ongoing, and significant contribution to one of higher education's main functions. Addressing issues of multiculturalism and gender equity in a responsible and committed fashion can provide an excellent opportunity for athletics to display leadership on a societal issue that is becoming increasingly important. Rethinking an athletic department's financial relationship with the institution will enable the above-mentioned initiatives to become reality.

In many locker rooms, coaches prominently display the following, time-worn coaching adage, "There is no 'I' in 'TEAM.'" Coaches cite this phrase to convey to their student-athletes the notion that the needs and goals of the individual are never greater than those of the team. It is time for athletic leaders themselves to prove that they know how to be team players. Thus, the challenge is to reconsider each and every athletic department function to determine if that function can be carried out in a way that will improve the welfare of the team—in this case higher education. So at a time when all components of the higher education enterprise are being challenged to demonstrate that what they do contributes in direct and meaningful ways to broader institutional goals, athletics must do the same. In short, if we are to achieve the New Standard, athletic departments and all who work in them must become "a part of, rather than apart from" the university.

References

Acosta, R. Vivian, and Linda Jean Carpenter. 1996. *Women in Intercollegiate Sport: A Longitudinal Study, 1977-1996.* Department of Physical Education, Brooklyn College, Brooklyn NY.

Berkow, Ira. *The New York Times.* 30 March 1992.

Bok, Derek. 1990. *Universities and the Future of America.* Durham, NC: Duke University Press.

College Football Association. 1987. *Profile of the College Viewer.* Conducted by Simmons Market Research Bureau, Inc. Information provided in 15 July 1996 phone conversation with Chris Kiser of the CFA.

Giamatti, A. Bartlett. 1988. *A Free and Ordered Space: The Real World of the University.* New York: W. W. Norton.

Hudson Institute and U.S. Department of Labor. 1987. *Workforce 2000.* Washington, DC: Government Printing Office.

Knight Foundation Commission on Intercollegiate Athletics. 1991. *Keeping Faith with the Student-Athlete.* Charlotte, NC: Knight Foundation.

National Association of Athletics Compliance Coordinators. 1995. "Final Television Survey Results In." *NAACC Quarterly* 9 (5).

National Collegiate Athletic Association. 1991. *The Public and the Media's Understanding and Assessment of the NCAA.* Pole conducted by Louis Harris & Associates, New York: NCAA.

National Collegiate Athletic Association. 1994. *NCAA Minority Opportunities and Interests Committee's Four-Year Study of Race Demographics of Member Institutions.* Overland Park, KS: NCAA.

National Collegiate Athletic Association. 1996. *1996 NCAA Division I Graduation Rates Report.* Overland Park, KS: NCAA.

NBC Sports. 6 August 1996 media release.

The New York Times. Reader Panel Section Readership Study. New York: Hughes Research, 1995.

Schultz, Richard D. 1991. "1991 NCAA State of the Association Address." 7 January. Nashville, TN.

Tinto, Vincent. 1993. *Leaving College: Rethinking the Causes and Cures of Student Attrition.* Chicago: The University of Chicago Press.

Torpor, Bob. 1995. "Athletics and Marketing." *Marketing Higher Education.* March Vol. IX, No.3. Torpor & Associates. Mountain View, CA.

Wingspread Group on Higher Education. 1993. *An American Imperative: Higher Expectations for Higher Education.* Racine, WI: The Johnson Foundation.

Zenith Media Services, Inc. 1997. March 13, Memo from Craig Jaffer, Research analyst. (New York).

PART THREE

· · · · · · · · · · · · ·

The Future

CHAPTER 8

Legislating for the Student-Athlete

Protecting the interests of the student-athlete must be the first priority when discussing recruiting guidelines.

Jamila Wideman
"A Ringing Endorsement of Phone Restrictions"

The primary thrust of this book is to challenge the higher education community to rethink the role of athletics in higher education using the New Standard. As explained in Chapter 1, the athletic community has lost sight of the primary purpose of athletics conducted within an educational setting. Therefore, the initiatives outlined in the preceding pages have been largely of a broad and philosophical nature. But for athletics to reach its full potential to contribute to higher education's mission in meaningful ways, philosophical change should be followed by specific legislative changes. The purpose of this chapter is to outline a few specific NCAA rule changes that will contribute to the effort to meet the New Standard.

A word of caution is in order. The specific legislative changes proposed in this chapter are only a sampling of rules that could be amended to help meet the New Standard. One of the great misconceptions regarding athletic reform is that it can be achieved through a laundry list of specific rule changes. There have been rule changes, for example, that have improved student-athlete welfare, but approaching reform in this way can result in missing the educational forest because of the legislative trees. As a former NCAA legislative assistant, I am well aware of how easy it is to become lost in the legislative minutia that is the NCAA Manual, all 579 pages of it. That is why the change necessary for athletics to justify its place in higher education must first occur at the philosophical level. From that point, specific legislative changes can be implemented. Attacking the problem in a whirlwind of specific, patchwork legislative initiatives without clear philosophical reference points only results in a fragmented, increasingly complex, and ever-changing manual.

RULE MAKING THAT IS STUDENT-ATHLETE CENTERED

The scene was the floor of the 1990 NCAA Convention, and the delegates, numbering more than 2,000, were discussing one of the 130 proposed rule changes on the agenda. A young man approached one of the floor microphones, identified himself as a student-athlete and a representative of the NCAA Student-Athlete Advisory Committee, and asked to address the convention. The delegation grew quiet. No one had ever seen a student-athlete address the convention regarding a specific NCAA rule proposal. It had only been a year since the membership had voted to create a student-athlete advisory committee. The occasion was, indeed, historic. Unfortunately, it was a bit of history the NCAA would rather have done without.

The student-athlete began to speak. The NCAA officials and officers on the dais, however, appeared confused as they hurriedly conferred. Before the young man could outline the Student-Athlete Advisory Committee's position on the proposal at hand, the chair of the session interrupted and informed him that NCAA Convention rules of order prohibited a student-athlete from addressing the delegation. Needless to say, there were quite a few red faces in the room that day, and the policy was amended the following year. The irony, however, was striking.

For years, athletic directors and coaches have driven the NCAA's legislative agenda. They have rarely been challenged and have almost always been successful in implementing legislation favorable to their own interests. As outlined in Chapter 5, these interests are often at odds with those of student-athletes. Only recently have presidents fully exerted their influence in legislative matters. Even more recently, student-athletes have been provided the opportunity to access and influence the adoption of the rules that so greatly affect their lives. While these developments are positive, some rules still work against student-athletes' long-term academic and personal interests. To meet the New Standard, we must boldly amend such rules. But before we can consider the rules that need amending, we must change the criteria upon which NCAA rules are evaluated and adopted.

Many coaches and athletic administrators have advanced the notion that the fundamental criteria that should be used in the adoption of NCAA rules and policies should revolve around the personal welfare of the student-athlete. But the fundamental principle upon which all NCAA policies and rules should be considered is what is in the best *long-term* academic and personal interests of the student-athlete. In this case, the word "long-term" is defined as what is in the best interest of student-athletes for the next 50 years. To illustrate this point, consider the oft-claimed belief that student-athletes should be paid.

It is easy to think that paying student-athlete stipends will solve all their problems and those of college athletics as well, an easy solution for our quick-fix society. But if we had the long-term academic and personal interests of our student-athletes in mind, we would stop talking about paying them and begin identifying ways in which we can assure that they actualize the personal, academic, athletic, and economic opportunities afforded by an athletic scholarship. Specifically, our daily actions must show clearly that educating student-athletes is the primary purpose of our athletic departments and that the true measure of success hinges upon obtaining a degree. A monthly stipend lasts a month at best. A well-developed appreciation for learning and the value of a college degree will last a lifetime. Calling for the payment of student-athletes is not the answer: It only reinforces the myth that the road to economic and personal prosperity is best attained by chasing athletic fame, glory, and financial reward. Our task is to adopt policy that will better enable us to teach our student-athletes to prosper so they will be able to live fulfilling lives.

Numerous rules, ranging from practice restrictions to eligibility to financial aid, serve the interests of the athletic department over the interests of the student-athlete. This is not surprising given the fact that NCAA rules have always been proposed, evaluated, and voted upon by members of the athletic establishment, with no input from student-athletes.

Because it has been coaches and athletic administrators who have driven the rule-making process, one of the major considerations when evaluating rules has been concern regarding competitive equity, or as more commonly understood, "leveling the playing field." Simply put, the fear that a competitor might gain a slight advantage has prevented the adoption of rules that would benefit the student-athlete. But as Cedric Dempsey, executive director of the NCAA expressed in his 1997 "State of the Association" address, "This concept [building a level playing field] has helped intercollegiate athletics because it has meant more parity in competition. But in the end, we can never achieve a truly level playing field."

What Dempsey says is true. The fear that a particular rule will suddenly shift the tilt of the playing field or radically alter the current balance of power in college athletics is unfounded. An excellent example of this can be found in the area of recruiting. Representatives of the "powerful" schools may not want to see a major change in recruiting rules because departure from the status quo threatens their level of success on the field. Coaches of schools not considered national powers would prefer to lengthen recruiting calenders and increase contacts so they can make up for what they lack in national visibility through perseverance and hard work. However, regardless of the changes that occur in recruiting, the same schools will continue to dominate on the fields and on the courts.

In football, for example, virtually the same group of teams have been ranked in the UPI's top 20 for the last 30 years. Of the top 20 ranked teams in 1968, 10 were in the top 20 in 1974, 9 in 1985, and 9 in 1995. Scattered throughout the remainder of the top 20 were another 20 or so schools that simply shuffled in and out of the rankings. NCAA recruiting, eligibility, and practice rules have changed dramatically since 1968, but for the most part, the football powers have remained the same. Regardless of the rule changes, traditional football powers such as Notre Dame, Alabama, and Penn State will remain traditional powers, as will North Carolina, Kentucky, and Kansas in basketball.

Nor is the fear that a particular change will result in an increase in cheating, an acceptable excuse to justify not adopting rules that are student-athlete centered. Rules should be adopted with the assumption that they will be followed rather than circumvented or ignored. As with any rule, the potential for abuse exists. Those who will abuse a new rule are likely to be the same people who have been abusing the current rules. One of the great injustices in college athletics is that rules have become far too restrictive; as they stand, they penalize the majority for the misdeeds of the few. Change that will benefit the majority of student-athletes and coaches with integrity should not be resisted simply because of the paranoia of a few and the dishonesty of even fewer.

One needs to look no further than the previously mentioned discussion amongst the Southeastern Conference athletic directors concerning the proposal to loosen the conference's transfer regulations to find an example of how rules have been adopted with minimal consideration for the welfare of the student-athlete. The athletic directors approached the issue solely from the standpoint of economics and competitive equity. They did not want to spend a significant amount of money recruiting a prospect only to compete against him the following year. This argument, as well as the fear that coaches would "tamper" with student-athletes at rival schools, carried the day. Student-athlete rights, however, were not mentioned in the discussion. Again, the way in which the athletic directors approached the issue is not a reflection on their integrity or character; it is simply a result of the realities of major college athletics. Due to the pressure to win and to balance budgets, athletic directors and coaches are forced to approach issues from the standpoint of economics and competitive equity.

Finally, for rules to meet the long-term interests of student-athletes, they must allow coaches to fulfill their educational responsibilities. NCAA legislation must contribute to the restoration of the "coach as educator" model. Similar to rules that work against the long-term academic and personal development of the student-athlete, some NCAA rules and policies actually prevent coaches from becoming more integrated into the mainstream academic community (e.g., the issue of restricted-earnings coaches versus graduate assistant coaches mentioned in Chapter 6). Those same rules discourage the athletic community from engaging in behavior that promotes educational achievement and student-athlete welfare. Described below are only a few examples of such rules, as well as suggestions for their amendment.

ELIMINATION OF THE ATHLETIC SCHOLARSHIP

At first glance, eliminating athletic scholarships in favor of a need-based formula would not appear to be in the best interest of student-athletes. However, if this proposal is judged upon what is in the best interest of student-athletes for the next 50 years rather than the four or five years they are on campus, it becomes clear that eliminating the athletic grant will contribute significantly to improving the student-athlete's chances of obtaining a well-balanced academic, personal, and athletic experience while in college.

The athletic scholarship provides coaches a tremendous amount of leverage over student-athletes, particularly as it applies to student-athletes' efforts to explore or develop nonathletic interests. Athletic departments view scholarship student-athletes as pieces of property, bought and paid for with an *athletic* scholarship. If, in the opinion of a coach, a student-athlete becomes too involved in "outside" interests, the coach makes it abundantly clear to the student-athlete that the athletic department signs the tuition check. A scholarship is a powerful means of keeping student-athletes focused upon athletic performance. A need-based financial aid system would result in student-athletes feeling less beholden to athletic departments and thus freer to explore the wide diversity of experiences that college has to offer.

The athletic scholarship also contributes to the alienation of student-athletes from the general student body. Although some may view student-athletes as heroes, most view them not as classmates, but as mercenaries or hired guns. Many faculty also resent the awarding of institutional financial aid to individuals who display only minimal interest in achieving academic success, while talented students in their discipline go unrewarded or attend another institution because it has offered a more attractive financial-aid package. Much student-athlete alienation from the general campus community is caused by the athletes being bought and paid for by the athletic department.

Some coaches may object because they believe that the elimination of full athletic scholarships would harm the quality of the game and take away educational opportunities from thousands of young people. I do not believe this to be the case. The quality of the game will remain virtually the same because those who wish to play athletics after high school have nowhere else to play (baseball being a notable exception). In football and basketball, such a change may make the games more attractive to a public that is increasingly skeptical about the student part of the student-athlete ideal. The public might actually enjoy watching competition between young people who they believe are truly part of the student body rather than hired mercenaries. Regarding the loss of educational opportunity, if a prospect was one that previously would have been awarded an athletic scholarship, the institution would see to it that his or her full financial need was met. Thus, the only loss of "opportunity" would be the opportunity for parents to save the difference in cost between a full and a need-based scholarship.

A need-based aid approach would also save money that could be used to increase athletic opportunities for women as required by Title IX or could be plowed into the university's general scholarship fund. According to an NCAA survey conducted in 1995, *Revenues and Expenses of Intercollegiate Athletics Programs: Financial Trends and Relationships,* 17 percent of Division I-A, 24 percent of I-AA, and 28 percent of I-AAA athletic department budgets are allocated for grants-in-aid. With only 28 percent of Division I programs operating in the black (Fulks 1995, 25, 39, 53), such a potential cost-savings measure should be seriously considered. This call to eliminate the athletic scholarship is even more timely now that the NCAA has adopted legislation to permit student-athletes to work during the academic year. This change, which was adopted during the 1997 convention, will allow student-athletes to earn money up to the school's full cost of attendance, thus offsetting any loss of scholarship money. While the additional burden of possibly having to obtain a job to offset a scholarship reduction might present hardships in the short run, it will have a long-term benefit, given the fact that student-athletes often have problems explaining their limited or nonexistent work experience to potential employers after their playing days are over.

A need-based financial aid formula, coupled with the opportunity to earn additional employment income, will result in a more independent and personally responsible student-athlete. Traditionalists will argue that such a change will open the door for schools to gain a competitive advantage by constructing "creative" need packages and offering better paying jobs. Some abuses will occur, but that possibility exists with any rule. As long as the student-athlete receives the going rate for work actually performed and he or she remains on track to graduate, why should any person be penalized because the "adults" associated with the program are dishonest? And who is to say that the practice of boosters overpaying student-athletes is not occurring in current summer jobs programs? As is now the case with summer jobs, the institution will be responsible for monitoring the employment arrangement.

Here again, the deeper concern of coaches is loss of control. Despite how beneficial such job experience might be or how needy the student, another outside responsibility will distract from what, in the coach's mind, should be the student-athlete's primary interest—athletic performance. Most coaches would rather provide student-athletes a full athletic scholarship along with a financial stipend, not necessarily because they are concerned about their financial situation, but because such an arrangement will allow "their athletes" to concentrate more fully on their athletic responsibilities.

For the vast majority of student-athletes, however, such a change will release them from what often amounts to excessive athletic department influence and oversight. The increased independence that will result from these changes will serve to develop student-athletes' sense of personal responsibility; enhance their ability to achieve a well-balanced athletic, academic, and social experience; and better prepare them to function as responsible citizens after their playing days are over.

FRESHMEN INELIGIBLE

In 1972, NCAA rules were changed to permit freshmen to play football and basketball at the varsity level. (Freshmen in all other sports have been eligible for varsity competition since 1968.) While the primary reason for this change was economic (maintaining freshmen teams is expensive), competing at the varsity level while performing successfully in the classroom was at that time a realistic expectation. Many freshmen have handled the difficult balancing act of academics and major college athletics. I was one of them. As a freshman at Davidson College, I was a starter on the basketball team and met the challenge of a difficult curriculum.

But that was in 1975, a long time ago. College athletics has changed dramatically since then. Flying coast-to-coast to play in "made for TV" games, with shoe companies and corporate sponsors investing millions of dollars in athletic programs, with coaches feeling the pressure to win games to retain their six-figure compensation packages, and with the white-hot media glaring at every turn, the pressure on today's student-athletes to perform is incredible. It is a lot farther from Podunk High to major college athletics than it used to be.

Some contend that making freshmen ineligible represents a denial of the basic right to participate in an extracurricular activity. But major college athletics has become anything but an ordinary extracurricular activity. It can be argued that exposing a 17- or 18-year-old to the high pressure and high visibility world of major college athletics while expecting that youngster to adjust to college both socially and academically is denying an even more fundamental right—the opportunity to earn a well-balanced academic, social, and athletic experience. Providing freshmen the chance to get their feet on the ground academically and socially and to sample fully the broad range of activities a college campus offers will go a long way in enabling student-athletes to realize that opportunity for success.

There have been other developments in college athletics over the last decade that make the timing right for a change. NCAA standards of continuing eligibility or satisfactory progress have been tightened significantly. These standards are now tied to grade point average and credit hours required for graduation. It is now far more difficult for student-athletes to maintain eligibility by enrolling in "crib" courses that do not lead toward a degree.

The elimination of initial eligibility standards may mean that colleges will admit more academically underprepared freshmen as "special admits." This is currently being done through the junior college system anyway. High school prospects who fail to meet NCAA initial eligibility standards are "farmed out" to junior colleges and after two years of usually suspect academic remediation are admitted to four-year institutions as transfers. Most directors of student-athlete support programs and faculty athletic representatives would argue that it is far more beneficial for freshmen, even marginally prepared "special admits," to enroll in a four-year college, become familiar with the campus and faculty, and avail themselves of the academic support programs on that campus than to attend a junior college, only to transfer two years later.

Coaches and athletic administrators from both two- and four-year institutions view junior college transfers differently from student-athletes who enroll in an NCAA institution directly from high school. Because most will be in the athletic program for only two years, junior college transfers are viewed not as students or even student-athletes, but rather as *athletic* "quick fixes." If a team has an immediate athletic need, whether it be a cornerback in football or a point guard in basketball, the coach turns to the junior college system to fill that need. To put it in stark terms, as in any business, more care and interest will be given to a four- or five-year investment than to a two-year investment.

Undoubtedly, the NCAA's establishment of initial eligibility standards for freshmen represented a bold academic statement in 1983. While it continues to be a statement, it is no longer bold enough, particularly in today's world where athletics are wildly overemphasized in comparison with academics. Freshman ineligibility may be the strongest statement educational leaders can make regarding our society's overemphasis on athletics at the expense of academic achievement. This change will send the message that there is more to life than athletics, a message that far too many student-athletes learn too late in life. Only when student-athletes (even those who are considered "can't miss pro prospects") learn this lesson can they begin preparing for a productive life after their playing days are over. The first step in that long and difficult process is to learn how to function when athletics are not the all-consuming interest in their lives. Although student-athletes who have worked hard and performed well academically at the high school level will be penalized, freshman ineligibility is in the long-term best interest of all student-athletes.

There is more to the story. According to the NCAA's Initial Eligibility Clearinghouse, the number of high-school grade-change waiver requests, initial eligibility waiver requests, nonstandard tests for students with learning disabilities, and nonstandard core course review requests has risen dramatically in the last year. For example, the clearinghouse received 100 grade-change waiver requests in 1995-96, up from fewer than 10 in 1994-95. Initial eligibility waiver requests were up from fewer than 200 in 1994-95 to over 350 in 1995-96. And 1,000 nonstandard tests for students with learning disabilities and 200 nonstandard core course review requests were considered in 1995-96 whereas, in 1993-94, there was a total of 300 such requests (Baugh, Kingston, and Lindeman 1996). Further, the clearinghouse case volume is likely to increase even more significantly with the implementation of the tightened initial eligibility standards in 1996-97.

Could it be that high school and college coaches along with high school teachers and principals are figuring out ways to beat the NCAA's initial eligibility system through the waiver process? Are we beginning to uncover the all too familiar pattern of bending rules for the short-term athletic gain of the student-athlete and economic gain of the institution at the expense of what is in the long-term educational best interest of the student-athlete? While there is no way to tell for certain, this significant increase in waiver requests and nonstandard tests for learning disabled prospects is disturbing.

Finally, making all freshmen ineligible for varsity competition would lay to rest the controversy over the use of standardized test scores to determine freshmen eligibility. This controversy has plagued the NCAA since the adoption of initial eligibility standards. The controversy centers upon the claim that the NCAA is in violation of Title VI of the Civil Rights Act of 1964, which bars racial discrimination by institutions that receive federal funds. The logic is that standardized tests are poor predictors of black students' performance, and therefore have a disproportionate effect on them.

Most important of all, the requirement that freshmen sit out of athletic competition will serve to slow down the big money, high visibility, and heavy pressure that college athletics brings. College athletics, particularly the sports of football and basketball, resembles a runaway freight train careening down the tracks, ever in danger of derailment. With larger and larger stakes being raised and more and more pressure on coaches to win games, student-athletes to perform well, and athletic directors to balance budgets, college athletics might be well served by taking a time-out. Things are moving way too fast. We are asking our student-athletes for far too much far too soon. Let's give them an opportunity to step back and take a deep breath so that they have a chance to notice the big, wide, and exciting world beyond the locker room—a world to which they will have to adapt to achieve success after their playing days are over.

THREE SEASONS OF COMPETITION WITH OPPORTUNITY TO EARN A FOURTH

Even a rule as basic as the number of seasons in which they are eligible to compete is flawed as it relates to the long-term interests of student-athletes. Currently, student-athletes who are qualifiers out of high school may participate in four seasons of competition. Nonqualifiers, however, after sitting out their initial year, may participate in three seasons of competition with the opportunity to earn a fourth season if they graduate after their fourth year on campus. In either case, eligibility rules are based upon the assumption that a student will graduate in four years. While that may have been true in the past, according to the 1996 NCAA Division I Graduation Rate Report, student-athletes on the average take 4.8 years to graduate: this compares to 4.7 for students in general (National Collegiate Athletic Association 1996, 622). The days when college students earned their degrees in four years are largely a thing of the past. That being the case, NCAA eligibility standards should be adjusted to encourage student-athletes to remain on campus for five years.

Awarding three years of eligibility with an opportunity to earn a fourth based upon satisfactory completion of enough credit hours to place the student within one year of graduation will motivate student-athletes to perform well academically to be able to continue to perform athletically. This change, coupled with freshmen ineligibility, will result in student-athletes being on campus for a five-year period. Critics will argue that an extra year only prolongs the student-athlete's immersion in the pampered, fantasy world of college athletics. But if the end result is more student-athletes with degrees, it is well worth it.

JUNIOR COLLEGE TRANSFER ELIGIBILITY

NCAA rules governing junior college transfers, in particular, junior college transfers who were nonqualifiers out of high school, also serve the athletic department's short-term athletic needs rather than the student-athlete's long-term academic needs. If a nonqualifier enrolled in a four-year institution directly from high school, he or she would be prohibited from engaging in any athletic activities during the initial year of enrollment. The message here is clear: You did not take care of business academically while in high school; therefore, you cannot participate in athletics for a year.

This penalty can be "taken care of" by enrolling in a junior college, where the student-athlete is eligible to play athletics and will do so for two years. If the student graduates from the junior college and obtains a predetermined number of credit hours, he or she can transfer to a four-year institution and become immediately eligible. The student-athlete can play for four consecutive seasons (two at the junior college and two at the four-year school), thus skirting the only penalty (loss of opportunity to participate in athletics) serious enough to hammer home the point that academics are important.

A rule that would require junior college transfers who were nonqualifiers to serve an academic year of residence at the four-year institution, however, would be better for them in their long-term educational best interests. While some argue that such a rule would "punish" such student-athletes twice, the fact remains that they are never required to serve the penalty of having to sit out a year athletically. Without this year of residence, these students are able to use four years of eligibility in four years. They just keep on playing, once again reinforcing the message that if you are good enough athletically, we will "take care of you."

Of any student likely to need five years rather than four to graduate, it would be one who struggled academically in high school. The required year of residence forces the nonqualified junior college transfer to remain on campus for five years to complete the allotted four years of eligibility. But as mentioned in the discussion of freshman eligibility, coaches enjoy having the opportunity to recruit a "quick athletic fix"—a mature player who can step in and immediately fill an athletic need. Once again, short-term athletic needs override what is in the long-term academic best interest of the student.

Actually, if all freshman were ineligible and then permitted three seasons of competition with the opportunity to earn a fourth as previously suggested, all junior college transfers should be required to sit out their first year at the four-year institution. The combination of these rules would require all student-athletes to remain on campus for a minimum of four-and-a-half years in the case of fall sport participants and five years in the case of those who participate in spring sports if they wished to complete their eligibility.

ELIMINATION OF OUT-OF-SEASON PRACTICE, INCLUDING SPRING FOOTBALL

Whatever happened to the off-season? And isn't the term "out-of-season practice" an oxymoron? "Out-of-season" should mean what it implies—no practice! Intercollegiate athletics is supposed to be an extracurricular activity. The term "student-athlete experience" suggests a balance between academics and athletics. NCAA rules regarding out-of-season practice, however, have sent the clear message that athletics is a full-time, year-round commitment and hardly extracurricular.

It is certainly reasonable to demand a sizable time commitment from student-athletes during the season, but not during the off-season. Current NCAA rules permit eight hours per week of conditioning and skills instruction supervised by the coaching staff. This rule was adopted because coaches were demanding far too much time from student-athletes in what was supposed to be the off-season. According to the results of a 1988 NCAA-sponsored study, student-athletes in the sports of football and basketball were, on average, spending 17.9 hours per week on activities related to athletics in the off-season. Student-athletes in other sports were spending 15.6 hours per week, compared to an average of 11.4 hours per week spent by other students in their chosen extracurricular activity (National Collegiate Athletic Association 1988).

While the eight-hour rule has sent the message that coaches must be more respectful of their student-athletes' time, it is arguable whether its intent is being fulfilled. This concern exists because student-athletes are permitted to engage in an unlimited amount of "volunteer" activities, such as weight lifting. Such "voluntary" activities are not counted in the eight-hour-per-week limitation. Unfortunately, coaches have taken advantage of these "voluntary" workouts to the point where the workouts are now actually mandatory. If you want to get a cynical laugh out of major college student-athletes, ask them about their "voluntary" workouts, both out-of-season and in-season, where the weekly limit is 20 hours.

Sports seasons can last more than five months. In an academic year that generally lasts only eight months, isn't that enough? In some sports, most notably football and basketball, student-athletes are expected to remain on campus during the summer to work out. When do these student-athletes get the chance to spend time the way an ordinary student does?

Spring football practice offers the best example of athletics becoming a year-round commitment. While coaches claim that it is the only time they get to concentrate on teaching the fundamentals of tackling and blocking and on trying out new players, the fact is, it's the first opportunity to begin the brutal and physically demanding tryout and weeding out process in preparation for the fall season. According to statistics compiled over the last six years through the NCAA Injury Surveillance System, the injury rate for spring practice is more than double the fall practice injury rate. "This result is even more alarming, when it is considered that the 15 spring practices are spread over 29 days, leaving plenty of recovery time (as compared to the fall), and that five of the spring practices are designed as non-contact" (Bunce and Wilson 1996, 4).

Given these statistics, spring practice comes to be more about determining just how "tough" players are and how much punishment they can take than about teaching them the fundamentals. More disturbing is the fact that the types of injuries sustained are more severe. Concussions more than double those sustained in the fall. The anterior cruciate injury rate is more than three times as bad. And injuries requiring surgery occur in spring at a rate of more than three times that of fall practice. Not only can an issue be made of the time demands required during spring practice, but one cannot help questioning the wisdom of exposing student-athletes to the chance of injury in the off-season two or three times as great as that of the regular season. For these reasons, spring football practice should be eliminated.

Coaches often contend that their student-athletes actually want to be coached by them year-round. I doubt it, at least not any team that I played on. Although we worked out on a regular basis in the off-season, we welcomed the opportunity to do so without the presence of coaches. Those student-athletes who are driven to work out all hours of the day, all year long, in the hopes of playing professionally, are obviously motivated enough to do it by themselves, without the coach demanding it or supervising their activities. Why should teammates who want to take time off to rest their bodies or simply to pursue other interests be held hostage because of the desires of coaches and of those few student-athletes who live and breathe athletics? Student-athletes are not professional athletes. College is an opportunity to explore a wide range of interests. We are denying student-athletes the opportunity to expand their interests by demanding excessive time commitments for athletics. In the off-season, student-athletes should be allowed to work out on their own and according to their particular level of interest and commitment without coaching pressure or supervision.

As much as coaches will complain, they would have no one else to blame but themselves if such rules ever passed. Coaches have lost sight of the fact that although athletics is a full-time job for them, it must be a part-time job for student-athletes. And as if this violation of student-athletes' rights is not bad enough, the lessons that are taught—that rules are made to be stretched and broken—raise serious questions about the educational benefits of college athletics.

MANDATORY DAY OFF

Another example of a rule that serves the athletic department's interests at the expense of student-athletes' time is the stipulation that allegedly provides student-athletes one day per week during which they are not required to engage in athletically related activities. This rule, adopted in response to the previously cited NCAA study that revealed the inordinate amount of athletically related time required of student-athletes, was hailed as a significant victory for student-athlete welfare. The victory, however, was short-lived.

Athletic department officials soon discovered that to meet the intent and true spirit of this rule, it would require more effort, creativity, and flexibility on their part in the areas of practice, contest, and travel scheduling than they were anticipating. Consequently, the rule was soon revised to permit team travel on this supposed "off" day. Team travel, it was said, would not be considered "an athletically related activity" for purposes of this rule. But team travel is definitely required, it is undoubtedly athletically related, and it certainly requires time. One day off per week should mean one day off per week from all athletically related activities. Once again, the interests of the student-athletes became secondary to those of the coaches and administrators. While this one day may not seem significant, it is, for it sends the clear message that athletics is a full-time, seven-day-a-week job.

ONE-TIME TRANSFER PROVISION TO APPLY TO ALL SPORTS

NCAA transfer rules are also stacked against the student-athlete. Currently, student-athletes in the sports of football, basketball, and ice hockey are required to serve a one-year residency upon transfer. In other sports, student-athletes are permitted to transfer without penalty on one occasion. While this rule is not one that will have a long-term effect upon student-athletes, it bears mention because it denies the student-athlete a funda-mental right enjoyed by all other students. A student on a music scholar-ship, for example, is not prohibited from participating in band activities after transferring to a new school. The identical economic and competitive arguments used to restrict transfer opportunities on the national level were used in the SEC. Both of these arguments are a thinly veiled attempt to divert attention from the real issue, which is, once again, control over what is considered athletic department "property." The first argument (fear of being defeated by a former student-athlete) is purely selfish, and the second (tampering by coaches) penalizes the student for the unethical behavior of adults.

Why shouldn't student-athletes be permitted to transfer without pen-alty, particularly when their scholarship agreement with the institution is only a one-year deal? Until scholarships are awarded for four- or five-year terms, athletic departments have no business denying student-athletes the opportunity to transfer and become immediately eligible. The most com-pelling argument for this change was articulated during a meeting of the Southeastern Conference Student-Athlete Advisory Committee. After explaining the reason for the transfer restriction, a student asked, "Why is it that coaches can change schools, and double their salary as well as go on coaching the next year? If we are required to sit out, shouldn't coaches, who have recruited many of us with the promise that they will be around for four years, be held to the same standard"? Case closed.

FOOTBALL SCHOLARSHIP LIMITATIONS

This is an example of a rule that works against football coaches fulfilling their academic responsibilities to student-athletes. Currently, Division I-A football teams may have no more than 85 student-athletes on scholarship at any one time. There is also a limit of 25 on the number of initial, or new, scholarships that can be awarded each year. Most Division I-A football programs redshirt a large number of freshmen, thus requiring most student-athletes to remain in the program for five years to complete their four years of eligibility. Simple math reveals that 25 scholarships per year stretched over a five-year period total up to 125 potential scholarship student-athletes moving through a program every five years. Yet, there can be no more than 85 scholarship football student-athletes on the squad list at any one time, potentially leaving 40 student-athletes, or 32 percent of those who enter the program, who must be "eliminated" from the program over that five-year period. The rule actually forces significant program attrition.

Coaches like the rule because it provides a greater margin of error in recruiting. If a prospect does not meet expectations, he can easily be replaced. The rule also permits coaches to recruit a greater number of "at-risk" student-athletes, because if they fail academically, the program is not penalized. Clearly, the current rule works against institutional retention and graduation efforts.

A more sound approach academically would be to eliminate the overall cap and allow 20 initial scholarships per year with no opportunity to replace student-athletes who fail academically or drop off the team. This approach rewards retention. Some contend that this arrangement would raise costs due to the potential for a program to carry 100 scholarship student-athletes at one time. This argument is spurious because there will always be natural attrition; therefore, the likelihood of having 100 student-athletes on scholarship is minimal. Because football is, in large part, a game of depth and numbers, the rule would motivate coaches to take a more active interest in the academic welfare of their student-athletes. Coaches with high retention rates would, and should, be rewarded.

ELIMINATING OFF-CAMPUS RECRUITING

Some changes, if made, would promote the more effective integration of coaches into the mainstream university community. The most controversial, but undoubtedly the most effective, would be to eliminate off-campus recruiting, permit coaches to work out prospects during official visits, and extend the official visit from 48 hours to 60 hours. In many cases, athletic programs spend more money recruiting a blue-chip prospect than they do in hiring a new president. In today's world of videotape and independent scouting services, off-campus recruiting is no longer necessary. It is true that coaches are able to judge talent more precisely if they can observe prospects in person; however, the benefit of fine tuning their athletic evaluation does not outweigh the expense necessary to do firsthand recruiting. Using recruiting services and video, coupled with allowing prospects to be worked out during official visits, will enable coaches to adequately determine athletic ability.

But what about character? It is helpful to visit the prospect at home to get a feel for his or her family environment and possibly to pick up on any major personality flaws. And yes, coaches are being held more accountable for the types of student-athletes they are recruiting. But if a coach cannot get the sense of the personality and character of a young person through multiple telephone calls to the prospect, his or her coaches, guidance counselors, and teachers, all in addition to a personal campus visit for a long weekend, then that coach might want to consider a new career. The fact is, many coaches are more than willing to recruit a prospect with suspect character references, if he has an outstanding jumpshot. So, the argument that this change would hamper a coaches' ability to adequately determine a recruit's character is suspect at best.

Eliminating off-campus recruiting would also greatly deregulate the NCAA manual. Coaches and administrators are incessantly complaining about the overly thick and complex NCAA manual. Currently, the chapter devoted to recruiting comprises 44 pages, half of which would be eliminated by this change.

Most important, however, is the tremendous amount of time and resources devoted to recruiting. The task has come to overshadow the coach's primary role as an educator. Eliminating off-campus recruiting would allow coaches to spend more time teaching and mentoring their current student-athletes. It would also provide more opportunity for them to participate in the professional development or graduate school programs identified earlier. Many coaches lament the fact that they are no longer respected as educators. With the elimination of off-campus recruiting, the importance of hiring assistant coaches with strong skills in academics, mentoring, and coaching would increase as would the opportunity to become more integrated into the mainstream campus community.

As explained in Chapter 6, the increased emphasis on recruiting has had a significant effect on the academic and personal profile of college coaches. Just as this increased emphasis has resulted in a shift in the desired qualifications of assistant coaches from the teacher/educator to the recruiter/salesperson model, eliminating off-campus recruiting would have the effect of reversing this shift. This change would require coaches to be more astute judges of talent and character, a skill developed over years of coaching. Most college head coaches would trust the judgment of a coach with 10 years of head-coaching and classroom-teaching experience at the high school level more than that of a young coach formed in the recruiter/salesperson mold. This is particularly true when it comes to judging the intangibles of desire and character in a high school senior. Without the burden of traveling for the purpose of recruiting, many quality high school coaches, particularly veteran coaches with families who have had no interest in becoming college coaches, might now consider such opportunities. Thus, the elimination of off-campus recruiting would contribute in a significant way to restoring the "coach as educator" ideal.

Predictably, coaches may argue that this change will result in a diminished "product" on the field and court and that such a change eliminates the opportunity for them to "outwork" their rivals. But once again, these assertions are largely unfounded. The same number of prospects will attend and play for the same number of schools, and the same number of spectators will attend games and watch them on television. As for the concern about losing the opportunity to outwork their rivals, student-athletes and coaches themselves would be much better served if they became more concerned about outworking their rivals in providing educational leadership and guidance for student-athletes on campus than in flying all over the country wooing high school prospects.

Certainly there is the chance that eliminating off-campus recruiting will result in coaches making a few more recruiting mistakes. But the cost savings, the effect on the desired profile of assistant coaches, the increased involvement in mentoring enrolled student-athletes, and the chance to become more involved in the campus community far outweigh those few mistakes.

AMEND NCAA'S REVENUE DISTRIBUTION FORMULA

Another policy change that would encourage athletic departments to create an environment that promotes sound academic behavior from coaches has to do with the formula used by the NCAA to distribute revenue to its institutions. Because athletic departments are run as businesses and businesses are run to make money, the most effective way to influence departmental behavior is to offer financial reward for engaging in a desired behavior. Other than a number of fixed-sum grants provided to all institutions to cover the cost of catastrophic injury insurance and such, the NCAA distributes most of its revenue to member institutions based upon three factors: number of sports sponsored, number of scholarships offered, and athletic performance (conference performance in the NCAA basketball tournament over a rolling six-year period).

If higher education leaders wish to motivate athletic department officials to do a more effective job in educating their student-athletes, they should reward athletic departments financially for doing so. To that end, the athletic performance component of the NCAA revenue distribution formula should be eliminated and replaced with a graduation rate component. Programs that graduate student-athletes should be rewarded. Although graduation-rate calculation methods are not perfect, they continue to represent the most useful vehicle at our disposal for measuring an athletic department's academic commitment to its student-athletes. The concept is simple. Financial reward for desired behavior.

Some changes in the calculation formula are necessary, however. Universities should not be penalized for student-athletes leaving school early to play professional sports, provided they were on track to graduate when they left. Additionally, institutions should not be penalized because a student-athlete transfers, provided the student was on track to graduate at the time of transfer and graduates from the school to which he or she transferred.

COACHES' OUTSIDE VENTURES

While other rules could be amended to better accommodate the long-term academic and personal interests of student-athletes and help restore the "coach as educator" ideal, the final NCAA rule change discussed here involves the way in which coaches and, for that matter, all athletic department personnel are compensated from outside sources. A major contributing cause to the demise of the "coach as educator" ideal is the increased involvement of coaches in outside promotional activities that have little to do with teaching or education. Such involvement has left the impression that coaches are more about being entertainers and entrepreneurs than about being teachers and educators. Further, the significant income generated from endorsements—in many cases income that boosts coaches' salaries far beyond that of the institution's president—has further alienated the coach from the mainstream university community. And with so many outside commitments, how can coaches fulfill their primary educational and mentoring responsibilities to their student-athletes?

Currently, the NCAA requires that all athletic department staff members receive prior written approval from the institution's president for all athletically related income and benefits from outside the institution. While this stipulation represents progress, it must go further to require that all outside income earned as a direct result of the coach's position as an employee of the institution, particularly product endorsements, be directed through the university. The university can then choose to pay the coach whatever it deems appropriate.

Wilford Bailey and Taylor Littleton expressed their concern regarding the potential for conflicts of interest and the effect that involvement in outside ventures has on student-athletes. They suggested that coaches should be prohibited from "profiting personally from the use of university resources and not be permitted to engage in extramural activities that constitute a conflict of interest or a neglect of their institutional responsibilities, especially their role as 'teachers' in the comprehensive education of student-athletes. These are principles consistently applied for the approval of extramural activities for university faculty and staff, and they should be applied to coaches also. There is compelling logic in the argument that the replay of a university's football or basketball game on television is a part of the university's program and that revenue derived from it should accrue to the university rather than to the coach, and that when members of an athletic team wear a given brand of shoes any contribution from the manufacturer should come to the university for use in its program rather than to the coach" (Bailey and Littleton 1991, 127-28).

Obviously, coaches will not like this proposal, and they will likely cite faculty members who earn outside income from consulting or from securing research grants. But because faculty do it does not make it the right thing to do, particularly if it can be argued that their educational responsibilities, such as teaching, are not adequately being met. That notwithstanding, there is a significant difference between coaches endorsing products and faculty consulting. In the case of coaches, it is the *position* of head coach that generates a corporation's interest, not the particular talent or expertise. For coaches to think otherwise is pompous. If a coach leaves an institution, the next coach will receive a similar endorsement contract. Perhaps it will be from a shoe or apparel company because what attracts the advertisers in the first place is the access that hiring a coach gives them to his student-athletes' feet or the chance it gives them to sell the institution new uniforms, for the institution gets tremendous exposure on television and in pictures in magazines and newspapers, all of which are most attractive to advertisers. Other than in cases of the most visible and well-respected coaches, a Mike Krzyzewski or John Thompson, for example, once the coach leaves the institution, he is of little value to the advertiser.

It is a faculty member's *knowledge* or *expertise* that is of value to a corporation or a government agency. If a faculty member develops a process useful to a manufacturing company, the company will continue to compensate the individual regardless of whether he or she remains at the institution. Further, the company would not automatically request such services from, or provide such compensation to, a successor. Yes, the institution provides facilities for faculty to conduct research, but in the case of securing grants, the grant generally provides funding for the use of those facilities. Don't shoe companies provide shoes for the team? Yes, but it is the coach rather than the institution who receives the major share of the benefits. And in the case of endorsements for soft drinks, potato chips, and other nonathletic items, the institution receives virtually nothing. The intent of such a change is not to limit the amount of compensation a coach is able to earn. Rather, in cases where endorsement income is a direct result of the coach's being employed by the institution, the institution should realize the bulk of the financial reward.

A notable exception is sports camps. Coaches should continue to receive the proceeds from their sports camps, minus the normal facility rental expense, because in this case, the coaching staff is actually working for, conducting, and providing expertise that is of value to campers.

These are only a few NCAA and institutional rules and policies that work against the long-term academic and personal welfare of the student-athlete and the effective integration of the coach into the academic community. These rules and others have to be changed if we are to achieve our purpose of helping student-athletes and training coaches to be educators. To meet the New Standard, we must rethink the criteria upon which existing rules, in addition to those we will make in the future, are evaluated and adopted.

References

Bailey, Wilford, and Taylor Littleton. 1991. *Athletics and Academe: An Anatomy of Abuses and a Prescription for Reform.* New York: Macmillan.

Baugh, Robert, Jerry Kingston, and Charles Lindeman. 1996. Memorandum to NCAA Council titled "November 30, Summit Conference," January 1996.

Bunce, Donald, and Dennis Wilson. 1996. "Spring Practice Can Be a Safer Activity." *NCAA News,* 29 April.

Dempsey, Cedric. 1997. "1997 NCAA State of the Association Address." NCAA Convention, 12 January 1997, Nashville, TN.

Fulks, Daniel L. 1995. *Revenues and Expenses of Intercollegiate Athletics Programs: Financial Trends and Relationships.* Overland Park, KS: NCAA.

National Collegiate Athletic Association. 1988. *Studies of Intercollegiate Athletics Report No. 1.* Palo Alto, CA: American Institute for Research.

National Collegiate Athletic Association. 1996. *1996 NCAA Division I Graduation-Rates Report.* Overland Park, KS: NCAA.

National Collegiate Athletic Association. 1996. *1996-97 NCAA Manual.* Overland Park, KS: NCAA.

Wideman, Jamila. 1997. "A Ringing Endorsement of Phone Restrictions." *The NCAA News.* 6 January 1997, 4-5.

CHAPTER 9

The Challenge

Transformation of any sort—whether human or chemical or corporate—is a perilous passage at best, calling for a radical letting go, and an openness to the unknown. It's hard to imagine anything more frightening. And it's hard to find a likely route to progress—for in letting go of the old form we create the space for a new form that will work even better. It comes down simply to this: that we can't advance as long as we're holding tight to what no longer works. And we have to break the mold before a new form can emerge.

Margorie Kelly
"Taming the Demons of Change"

Coaches constantly instruct their players to recognize the parameters within which the game will be officiated and to be flexible enough to adjust their style of play to fit those parameters. For example, a basketball player who gets called for two early fouls because he aggressively "hand checks" an opponent had better rethink how to guard that opponent (stop hand checking!), or he will foul out of the game. Similar to the way in which athletes must adjust their style of play to correspond with how "tight" officials are calling a game, those involved in college athletics must understand the environment (rules, customs, and expectations) of the larger community (higher education) of which they are a part, as well as how that environment is changing.

The justifications we make to ourselves and the standard by which we judge success have remained virtually unchanged for close to a century. During this time, however, higher education and the society it serves have changed dramatically. Do the long-standing justifications and standards we have used need to be broadened in today's world? And should we continue to define success in a way that does not benefit our student-athletes in the long run? Critical evaluation is essential to ensure the future welfare of intercollegiate athletics because any organization that does not meet its stated objectives will eventually become ineffective and possibly obsolete. Athletics will serve a meaningful purpose on college campuses in the future only if we engage in a thorough and continual self-assessment of the relevance of our justifications to ourselves and the standard that we use to determine what is success and what is not.

PROSPECTS FOR CHANGE

Obviously, our efforts to implement the New Standard will have limitations. The demands of television and the influence of big money and a society that believes you must be number one or you are no one, are all powerful forces. Perhaps the most significant force is human nature itself. Working in college athletics is a nice deal. It is fun, it is exciting, and it is certainly gratifying to the ego to have your work covered in the newspapers and on national television. It can also can be a glamorous and lavish life-style with elaborate parties and dinners, meetings at swank resorts, and exciting travel to interesting places for games. A person can even earn a nice living in college athletics these days. In short, when part of the athletic establishment, it becomes easy to ignore or resist the need for change.

Undoubtedly, the changes proposed in this book will make many coaches and athletic administrators uncomfortable because the changes represent a significant departure from the way in which things have been done for a long time. There is also the fear that change will result in a significant shift in the balance of power in college athletics. For these and other reasons, change of the type proposed in this book is often dismissed by the athletic establishment as being completely unworkable, far too radical, and a threat to the survival of college athletics. And, as has always been the case, coaches and administrators will not be challenged to prove their assertions. But they must be challenged. We must all ask ourselves, "Why won't this change work? How do we know it won't work if we don't try to change?" With our society changing at such a rapid pace and higher education struggling to respond to those changes, justifying past practices simply on the basis that "we have always done it that way" or that "it might put us at a recruiting disadvantage" is no longer acceptable.

While our resistance to change is formidable, there are some fundamental principles and uncompromised truths upon which we should all be able to agree. A commitment not only to the athletic welfare, but more important, the academic and personal well-being of student-athletes seems to be a reasonable ideal. Expecting coaches and athletic administrators to act first and foremost as educators rather than entertainers and entrepreneurs is not unrealistic. After all, they are professionals employed by an educational institution. It is fair to expect that college athletic programs contribute in meaningful ways to the educational mission of the institution of which they are a part. While some may think these principles idealistic or unattainable, this book has outlined many things that we can do to move us closer to realizing our goals.

Further, there are some indications that meaningful change in the way athletic programs are conducted is possible. Without question, the potential for positive reform of intercollegiate athletics is greater today than at any other time. Other attempts at athletic reform have been made in the past. The first was in 1906, when the Intercollegiate Athletic Association of the United States was formed in response to President Theodore Roosevelt's call to reform the violent nature of football. (The 1905 season produced 18 deaths.) In 1910, the organization was renamed the National Collegiate Athletic Association. It was formed, however, to address the rules of the game of football only. It wasn't until the mid 1910s that the association became involved with establishing standards relating to amateurism.

The second major attempt at national reform came in the form of a report by the Carnegie Foundation for the advancement of teaching. While the report, released in 1929, identified some of the key problems in intercollegiate athletics (violations of amateurism principles, compromising of academic standards, etc.) as well as a key element of reform (presidential control), there was little in the way of sustained follow-up to its recommendations. Since then, the NCAA has made periodic efforts to address specific areas of concern, such as financial aid or recruiting. However, no other major effort at sweeping national reform has been undertaken until the current effort. This most recent effort began in earnest at the 1984 NCAA Convention with the establishment of the NCAA President's Commission.

What distinguishes this attempt at reform from previous attempts is that it continues to this day. It is significant that the effort has been sustained and even fueled by the collective efforts of college presidents. They overwhelmingly agree that too much emphasis is given to intercollegiate athletics at schools with big-time athletic programs. According to a 1990 Louis Harris & Associates survey, 77 percent of presidents indicated as much.

While past scandals have attracted the attention of presidents, the interest of presidents in initiating a sustained effort at meaningful reform had always been fleeting. Today, college presidents seem resolute in their desire to bring big-time college athletic programs under control. They believe they will be successful in their reform efforts. In that same survey, 83 percent indicated that "colleges and universities themselves will be able to bring big-time athletic programs under control and make them a part of the academic community" (Louis Harris & Associates 1990). For these significant reasons, the prospects for the types of change urged in this book are better than ever. The question is whether the higher education community will take advantage of the opportunity to implement them.

While presidential resolve remains the key ingredient for continued, meaningful reform, other factors will keep attention focused on the issue. The oft-mentioned decline in public trust in higher education, coupled with the problem of increasingly scarce resources for education, will raise the issue of athletics' contribution to the overall mission of the university to new levels. Additionally, the increased power and influence of the media, coupled with the continued public outcry over athletic scandals, will keep the issue of athletic department integrity front and center on higher education's agenda. Concern regarding how to assure that athletic programs become and remain an integral part of the higher education community will intensify.

IF CHANGE IS NOT REALIZED

The question now and in the future will be whether athletics is contributing to higher education's purpose in meaningful ways. Athletics' success in that regard has been uneven at best. With such results, the question then becomes, "If athletics has only mixed success in fulfilling its primary purposes, why have it as part of higher education?" If you think athletics will always be a part of higher education, think twice!

To think that major college athletics will continue to play its present role in higher education is naive. One only has to consider the following comments to draw the conclusion that athletics' heretofore unquestioned position within American higher education may be eroding.

Herbert London, then editor-in-chief of *Academic Questions* and currently chairman of the National Association of Scholars and a professor of Humanities at New York University, wrote the following in 1992-93:

> As the recent Olympics shows, the distinction between amateur and professional athletes is now hopelessly blurred. Perhaps a similar blurring among Division I athletic programs could have a salutary effect on degree requirements. Instead of vitiating degree standards to accom-

modate athletes, big-time sports programs should be disentangled from colleges. Let those who wish to play big-time sports become semiprofessionals attached in a contractual way to colleges. Let colleges charge for the use of their football field and gymnasia. And let academic programs retain their integrity without any concession to athletes.

If this proposal were adopted, the disparity in graduation rates would become irrelevant. There would be no need for Congressional oversight of big-time college sports. There would be no need for athletic scholarships. There would be no need for compromising admissions or graduation requirements. The adoption of this recommendation would eliminate the cynicism that now surrounds student-athletes and their "academic" programs. And finally, we would be able to address more honestly our responsibility to provide quality higher education to black Americans. (London 1992-93)

Alexander Wolff's feature in the 12 January 1995 edition of *Sports Illustrated,* entitled "Broken Beyond Repair," focused still more public attention on the issue of the separation of big-time athletics from higher education. In an open letter to University of Miami (Florida) president, Edward "Tad" Foote, Wolff claimed that the litany of NCAA rules violations, misconduct of players and coaches, boosters run amok, use of steroids, the cover-up of positive drug tests, academic fraud, and numerous displays of unsportsmanlike conduct had resulted in an unacceptable amount of bad publicity and that the athletic program represented a cancer that was devouring the institution.

Getting rid of football would help you achieve your goal of transforming Miami into a first-rate private university in an urban setting. Several studies have found that athletic success by itself has no effect on alumni giving. On the contrary, according to at least one study, when winning is accompanied by the outrages with which you have become all too familiar, football glory may actually discourage contributions. In 1986, the year after Tulane shut down its basketball program in the wake of a point-shaving scandal, donations to that school leaped by $5 million. Wichita State raised $26 million in a special drive in '87, the year in which it dropped football. In roughly the same period during which your football program dragged Miami's name through the mud, another urban, private university has gone big-time—raising huge amounts of money, going on a building binge and raiding the Ivy League for faculty—without big-time sports. And no one has any less respect for NYU because it doesn't field even a club football team. Other schools have abolished a major sport for far less cause than you have to do so right now. . . . So do it. . . . Embark immediately on a fund-raising drive; you'll be astonished at how many

alumni will open up their wallets in response to your courage. (Wolff
1995, 26)

In one of the more thoughtful analyses of the issue, Thomas Hearn,
president of Wake Forest University and a former member of the NCAA
Presidents Commission, spoke about the challenges facing the college
athletic community at the 1988 College Football Association's Annual
Meeting.

> The universities of America cannot and will not tolerate in their
> structure any element which contradicts their purpose. However much
> people may love football victories and create idols of coaches, the
> system of higher education will be purged of semiprofessional sports
> unless athletics can be made consistent with the moral and social
> responsibilities of universities. In North Carolina, when people have a
> serious purpose, the saying is, "When those guys go hunting, they carry
> guns." Well, there are guys with guns out there hunting big time
> college sports. If reform falters, they will shoot to kill. You are in their
> sights. The urgent question for you is whether your programs can be
> made to serve the larger purposes of universities. (Hearn 1988)

Many within the athletic community will dismiss these comments either
as inconsequential grumbling from deep inside the ivory tower or sensa-
tionalized attacks from the media. They are wrong to dismiss them. The
comments are pervasive and from high levels in the higher education
community. If athletics does not become more successful in effectively
contributing to the mission of the university, big-time sports could well be
severed from higher education. At the very least, it could be forced to
undergo a radical transformation. To dismiss totally what appears to be
growing discontent regarding athletics' place on campus is a mistake. This
"athletics hubris" only serves to further alienate coaches and athletic
administrators from the mainstream higher education community.

In today's environment of increasing financial pressure and decreasing
public trust, each and every university component is being scrutinized and
evaluated to determine its effectiveness in contributing to higher education's
purpose. To think that athletics is not going to be held to the same standard
of utility as other components of higher education is simply misguided.
Everyone involved in college athletics must fully understand that higher
education was around for more than 200 years before the first intercollegiate athletic contest and will continue to provide quality education,
produce meaningful research, and contribute to the betterment of society
with or without athletics. Further, American higher education is the only
higher education system in the world to so fully incorporate competitive
intercollegiate athletics into its formal structure. Thus, the challenge is not
to dismiss these concerns, but to address them directly. If athletics is not

fully realizing its potential to contribute to higher education's mission, we must rethink how it can do so.

WHY DO WE CARE?

You might ask, "Aren't you overreacting? Why can't you just relax and enjoy the games? Why should we care so deeply about whether athletics fits comfortably within higher education? After all, they are just games."

Bart Giamatti, the late president of Yale and the Commissioner of Major League Baseball, delivered a speech in 1987 at Williams College. It was entitled "The State of the College Game," and it most clearly articulated why we should care deeply about athletics fully meeting its potential to contribute to higher education's mission.

> Why do we care? What difference does it make if some 250 or 300 institutions abuse athletics and their own stated academic missions? After all, in the vast majority of America's 2,800 or so colleges and universities, thousands and thousands of students play sports at all levels for the joy of the competition itself and to the delight and pride of a local community: there are hundreds and hundreds of fine coaches in this country who in fact care deeply for their profession—which is a teaching one—for their institution's integrity, and for their athletes and their intellectual and moral well-being. There are high-quality athletics programs in colleges and universities that are well managed, successfully integrated into their academic communities and scandal free. Why do we care about the big time or the would be big time? Why not simply say, Let the bandits be bandits: the vast majority will survive.
>
> We care because all students are important—all young people are valuable—not simply our own. If all Americans should have the opportunity to pursue higher education, then *all*—not just most— should be given the chance to fulfill themselves as human beings. We care because we truly believe athletics plays a valuable role in an individual's education. Athletics can be a liberal pursuit, an activity pursued in and of itself, for the sheer joy of stretching the spirit as perhaps nothing else can. There are values (and we hear so much about values in education and how they are missing) the individual learns—of cooperation, fairness, dedication, discipline—as well as lessons about limitation and how to live with failure, that are valuable and necessary to learn for life. And we care not simply because individuals are important per se, or because athletics is a valuable part of education. We also care because the whole educational enterprise is connected, and it is wrong to say, Let them go; we will watch their banditry from our high place on the hill. It is important to care about

the state of athletics at the collegiate level because it is indissolubly linked, in the public mind, with education at the collegiate level.

Higher education will continue to exist and thrive with or without college athletics. Despite how many fans attend games or watch them on television, the English, history, and chemistry departments, and the faculty who teach and conduct research in those subjects, are linked far more intimately and contribute far more directly to the purpose of higher education than do the football, basketball, or tennis teams and the coaches and administrators who oversee them.

This scenario is already being played out at many high schools throughout the nation as taxpayers and secondary school administrators are less willing to subsidize sports programs at the expense of classroom instruction. High school students are now being assessed fees to participate in a sport, or in more severe cases, sports are being eliminated. Such practices were unimaginable only a decade ago. So as university budgets become tighter and resources more scarce, it is foolish to think athletics is untouchable and will always be around in more or less the same form as today. That being the case, while developing other components of its mission, educational leaders must at the same time aggressively pursue ways in which to improve athletics' effectiveness in meeting its current purposes. In short, college athletic programs must adopt the New Standard of success, a standard based not solely on wins and losses or championships won, but on how effective a program is in contributing to the institution's efforts to fulfill its mission.

TIME TO THINK AT A NEW LEVEL

The New Standard will take more than presidential resolve; it cannot be achieved solely through NCAA initiatives. Unfortunately, there exists a perception that the NCAA can address all that is wrong with intercollegiate athletics. Consequently, those involved in college athletics and higher education feel no individual responsibility to do their part to initiate the positive changes that virtually everyone knows must occur to fully reform intercollegiate athletics. While much can be accomplished by working through the NCAA, the organization is simply a vehicle through which colleges and universities can act in a collective fashion to address common concerns. Like the many and various instruments in an orchestra, it is the manner in which the musicians play them that makes beautiful music. Each individual in the orchestra has a personal responsibility to execute his or her musical assignment correctly, responsibly, and in a manner that contributes to the orchestra's overall sound.

Consequently, we must all accept personal responsibility for making our programs "about the student-athlete"; we must help restore the "coach as educator" model and insure that athletic programs are "a part of rather than apart from" the institution. To that end, we must use these principles as philosophical reference points against which to measure all athletic decisions and policies. If a policy or decision is in harmony with the three principles outlined in this book and it contributes to meeting the New Standard, it will be sound. If not, it must be scrutinized further and restructured so that it is sound. It is only when we embrace these broad uncompromised truths as our own that we will be able to conceive of and achieve the specific measures that will make the New Standard a reality.

We must accept the New Standard enthusiastically. It must be seized as an opportunity to regain lost focus and to strengthen athletics' position on campus. Athletics' place in the educational community is justified with claims that it teaches valuable life skills such as leadership and teamwork. Higher education leaders and more specifically those in the college athletic community must now step forward and provide the leadership necessary to implement the New Standard. Such leadership will require the courage to challenge many of the false ideals held sacred by fans, media, coaches, and athletic administrators. It will require courage to step forward to challenge the myth that winning is everything and that athletic participation, regardless of the environment within which it occurs, has positive educational value. It will take courage to confront those who believe and act as if athletics is bigger and more important than the institution of which it is a part.

Finally, despite what those who wish to maintain the status quo insist, there is nothing to indicate that college athletics' tremendous public appeal and capacity to generate revenue will diminish when we implement the New Standard. Making programs be "about the student-athlete" and rebuilding the "coach as educator" model will not result in a sudden decline in public interest and support. If our programs become a part of the university, there is nothing to suggest that their economic value will decrease. Our games will still be exciting and entertaining. Alumni and fans will continue to attend those games, and television networks will continue to televise them. If we achieve success as defined by the New Standard, public interest in and support of college athletics will increase as our programs come to stand for more than simply turning a buck, preparing the next generation of professional stars, and winning-at-all-cost. The result is that the value of athletics within higher education will rise substantially.

The change referred to in the preceding pages represents change at a far more fundamental, philosophical, and managerial level than all other attempts at reform have demanded. It is change for which each and every individual in American higher education, including those in athletics, must accept personal responsibility. As teachers, we are *all* responsible for being honest with student-athletes and ensuring that they have a voice. As educators, we are *all* responsible for helping create an environment where coaches are rewarded not only for athletic success but for their academic performance as well. As members of the higher education community, we are *all* responsible for making sure that the athletic department is a part of the university. Each and every one of us—from president to graduate assistant, provost to trainer, alumni director to athletic director, faculty member to football coach, trustee to tennis coach—must speak out against those who believe that winning is everything. We must be responsible citizens of a society in which athletic accomplishment is wildly overemphasized in relation to educational excellence. We must *all* accept the challenge of meeting the New Standard.

References

Giamatti, A. Bartlett. 1988. *A Free and Ordered Space: The Real World of the University*. New York: W.W. Norton.

Hearn, Thomas. 1988. Speech at 1988 College Football Association's Annual Meeting, Dallas TX.

Kelly, Margorie. "Taming the Demons of Change." *Business Ethics*. July/August 1993.

London, Herbert. 1992-93. "A Note from the Editor." *Academic Questions*, Winter, Vol. 6, No. 1.

Louis Harris & Associates. 1990. Survey Conducted for The Knight Foundation Commission on Intercollegiate Athletics.

Wolff, Alexander. 1995. "Broken Beyond Repair." *Sports Illustrated*, 12 June. Vol. 82, No. 23, p. 20–26.

BIBLIOGRAPHY

Acosta, R. Vivian and Carpenter, Linda Jean. 1996. *Women in Intercollegiate Sport: A Longitudinal Study, 1977–1996.* Department of Physical Education, Brooklyn College, Brooklyn, NY.

Adler, Patricia A. and Adler, Peter. 1991. *Backboards and Blackboards: College Athletes and Role Engulfment.* New York: Columbia University Press.

Alexander, Caroline. 1995. *Battle's End: A Seminole Football Team Revisited.* New York: Alfred A. Knopf.

Anderson, Martin. 1992. *Imposters in the Temple.* New York: Simon and Schuster.

Andre, Judith and James, David J. 1991. *Rethinking College Athletics.* Philadelphia: Temple University Press.

Bailey, Wilford and Littleton, Taylor. 1991. *Athletics and Academe: An Anatomy of Abuses and a Prescription for Reform.* New York: MacMillan Publishing.

Bok, Derek. 1986. *Higher Learning.* Cambridge, MA: Harvard University Press.

———. 1990. *Universities and the Future of America.* Durham, NC: Duke University Press.

———. 1982. *Beyond the Ivory Tower: Social Responsibilities of the Modern University.* Cambridge, MA: Harvard University Press.

Bradley, Bill. 1996. *Time Present, Time Past.* New York: Alfred A. Knopf.

Bunce, Donald and Wilson, Dennis. "Spring Practice Can Be a Safer Activity." *NCAA News,* 29 April 1996.

Byers, Walter. 1995. *Unsportsmanlike Conduct: Exploiting College Athletes.* Ann Arbor, MI: University of Michigan Press.

Carter, Stephen L. 1996. *Integrity.* New York: Basic Books.

Chu, Donald. 1989. *The Character of American Higher Education and Intercollegiate Sport.* Albany, NY: State University of New York Press.

Chu, Donald, Segrave, Jeffrey, and Becker, Beverly. 1985. *Sport and Higher Education.* Champaign, IL: Human Kinetics Publishers.

College Football Association. *Profile of the College Viewer.* Conducted by Simmons Market Research Bureau, Inc., 1987.

Covey, Stephen R. 1989. *The Seven Habits of Highly Effective People.* New York: Simon and Schuster.

Crosset, Todd W., Benedict, Jeffrey R., and McDonald, Mark A. "Male Student-Athletes Reported for Sexual Assault: A Survey of Campus Police Departments and Judicial Affairs." *Journal of Sport and Social Issues,* May, 1995, Vol. 19, No. 2.

Dempsey, Cedric. "1997 NCAA State of the Association Address." NCAA Convention, January 12, 1997, Nashville, TN.

Denlinger, Ken. 1994. *For the Glory.* New York: St. Martin's Press.

D'Souza, Dinesh. 1991. *Illiberal Education.* New York: The Free Press.

Falla, Jack. 1981. *NCAA: The Voice of College Sports.* Mission, KS: NCAA.

Fulks, Daniel L. 1995. *Revenues and Expenses of Intercollegiate Athletic Programs: Financial Trends and Relationships.* Overland Park, KS: NCAA.

Galbraith, John Kenneth. 1996. *The Good Society: The Humane Agenda*. New York: Houghton Mifflin Co.

Gerdy, John R. "Team Spirit, Let's Hear It: Coaches and Athletic Administrators Must Become Better Team Players in Institutional Advancement." *CASE Currents*, March, 1997, Vol. xxiii, No. 3.

———. "Athlete Welfare Part of International Control." *NCAA News*, 3 March 1997, Vol. 34, No. 9.

———. "Time Out for Freshmen Ineligibility." *The College Board Review*, November 1996, Vol. 179.

———. "Student-Athletes, the World Bank and the United Nations." *Black Issues in Higher Education*, 22 August 1996, Vol. 13.

———. "Excessive Zeal to Win a Loser for Athletes." *NCAA News*, 22 April 1996, Vol. 33, No. 16.

———. "Blow the Whistle on Athletics Coaches." *Trusteeship*, November/December 1995, Vol. 3.

———. "End Zone Celebrations Are Not the Real Problem." *The Sporting News*, 2 October 1995, Vol. 219, No. 40.

———. "Community Service and College Athletics: Justifying Athletics' Place on Campus." *Athletic Administration*, October 1995, Vol. 30.

———. "The Case Against Athletic Stipends." *The Sporting News*, 10 April 1995, Vol. 219, No. 15.

———. "A Deal That Works for Student-Athletes." *NCAA News*, 4 January 1995, Vol. 32, No. 1.

———. "How Televised Sports Can Further the Goals of Higher Education." *The Chronicle of Higher Education*, 7 December 1994, Vol. xli, No. 15.

———. "NCAA Presidents: Walking the Walk?" *NABC Courtside*, July-August 1994, Vol. 2, No. 8.

———. "You Reap What You Sow: Large Minority Student-Athlete Pool Not Effectively Utilized." *Black Issues in Higher Education*, 11 August 1994, Vol. 11, No. 12.

———. "Student-Athlete Development—An Institutional Responsibility." *The Academic Athletic Journal*, Spring 1994.

———. "An Assessment of the Educational Levels of NCAA Division I Coaches." *The National Review of Athletics*, January 1994, Vol. 1, No. 1.

———. "Restoring Trust in Higher Education: Athletics' Role." *The College Board Review*, Winter 1993-94, Vol. 170.

———. "What Is an 'Ethics Convention' About?" *NCAA News*, 22 November 1993, Vol. 30, No. 42.

———. "New Standards Require Planning." *NCAA News*, 2 November 1992.

———. "Faculty and College Athletics Reform: Seizing the Moment." *The Educational Record*, Summer 1992, Vol. 73.

———. "Rewriting Coach's Job Description." *Athletic Administration*, October 1991, Vol. 26, No. 5.

———. "A Proposal to Make '90's Decade of Student-Athlete." *NCAA News*, 10 September 1990, Vol. 27, No. 31.

———. "Cleaning the NCAA Slate: Compliance Framework Ensures Integrity." *Center for Study of Sport in Society Digest*, Fall 1990.

———. "NCAA Legislative Services: A Changing Image." *Athletic Administration*, December 1988, Vol. 23, No. 6.

————. "Should College Athletes Be Paid?" *The College Board Review,* Spring 1987, Vol. 143.

————. "No More Dumb Jocks." *The College Board Review,* Spring 1987, Vol. 143.

Gerdy, John R. and Estes, Lane. "An Assessment of the Educational Levels of NCAA Division I Coaches." *The National Review of Athletics,* January 1994.

Giamatti, Bartlett. 1988. *A Free and Ordered Space: The Real World of the University.* New York: W. W. Norton and Co.

Gilley, J. Wade. 1991. *Thinking About American Higher Education: The 1990's and Beyond.* New York: MacMillan Publishing Co.

Harris, Louis & Associates. 1995. *The Harris Poll, No. 17.* New York.

————. 1990. Survey Conducted for The Knight Foundation Commission on Intercollegiate Athletics. New York.

Hearn, Thomas. Speech at 1988 College Football Association's Annual Meeting, Dallas, TX.

Ingham, Alan G. and Loy, John W. 1993. *Sport in Social Development: Traditions, Transitions and Transformations.* Champaign, IL: Human Kinetics Publishers.

Isaacs, Neil, D. 1978. *Jock Culture U.S.A.* New York: W. W. Norton and Co.

Jackson, Phil and Delehanty, Hugh, 1995. *Sacred Hoops: Spiritual Lessons of a Hardwood Warrior.* New York: Hyperion.

Kelly, Margorie. "Taming the Demons of Change." *Business Ethics,* July/August, 1993.

Kerr, Clark. 1982. *The Uses of the University.* Cambridge, MA: Harvard University Press.

Kjeldsen, Eric. "The Manager's Role in the Development and Maintenance of Ethical Behavior in the Sport Organization." *Journal of Sport Management,* 1992, Vol. 6.

Knight Foundation Commission on Intercollegiate Athletics. 1991. *Keeping Faith with the Student-Athlete,* 1992, *A Solid Start: A Report on Reform of Intercollegiate Athletics,* 1993, *A New Beginning for a New Century.* Miami: Knight Foundation.

Lester, Robin. 1995. *Stagg's University: The Rise, Decline and Fall of Big-Time Football at Chicago.* Urbana, IL: The University of Illinois Press.

Lipsyte, Robert. "When 'Kill the Ump' Is No Longer a Joke." *The New York Times,* 19 January 1997, Sec. 8, pp. 1 and 4.1.

————. 1975. *SportsWorld: An American Dreamland.* New York: Quadrangle Press.

Michener, James, A. 1976. *Sports in America.* New York: Random House.

Micracle, Andrew and Rees, C. Roger. 1994. *Lessons of the Locker Room: The Myth of School Sports.* Amherst, MA: Prometheus Books.

Mrozek, Donald J. 1983. *Sport and the American Mentality 1880–1910.* Knoxville, TN: University of Tennessee Press.

National Association of Athletics Compliance Coordinators. "Final Television Survey Results In." *NAACC Quarterly,* Summer, 1995, Vol. 9.

National Association of College and University Business Officers. 1993. *The Financial Management of Intercollegiate Athletics Programs.* Washington, D.C.: NACUBO.

National Collegiate Athletic Association. *1996 NCAA Division I Graduation-Rates Report.* Overland Park, KS., 1996.

————. 1988. *Studies of Intercollegiate Athletics.* Palto Alto, CA, American Institutes for Research Report No. 1.

————. 1991. *The Public and the Media's Understanding and Assessment of the NCAA.* Conducted by Louis Harris and Associates. New York.

————. 1994. *NCAA Minority Opportunities and Interests Committee's Four-Year Study of Race Demographics of Member Institutions.* Overland Park, KS: NCAA.

————. 1996. *1996-97 NCAA Manual*. Overland Park, KS.

New York Times. Reader Panel Section Readership Study. Hughes Research, 1995.

Rosovosky, Henry. 1990. *The University: An Owners Manual*. New York: W. W. Norton and Co.

Rudolph, Frederick. 1990. *The American College and University: A History*. Athens, GA: University of Georgia Press.

Savage, Howard J., et al. 1929. *American College Athletics*. New York: Carnegie Foundation for the Advancement of Teaching.

Schultz, Richard D. 1991. NCAA State of the Association Address. Nashville, TN., 7 January 1991.

Sheehan, Richard G. 1996. *Keeping Score: The Economics of Big-Time Sports*. South Bend, IN: Diamond Communications.

Shields, David and Bredemeier, Linda. 1995. *Character Development and Physical Activity*. Champaign, IL: Human Kinetics Publishers.

Slaughter, John and Lapchick, Richard. 1989. *The Rules of the Game*. New York: MacMillan.

Smith, C. Fraser. 1992. *Lenny, Lefty and the Chancellor: The Len Bias Tragedy and the Search for Reform in Big-Time College Basketball*. Baltimore: The Bancroft Press.

Sperber, Murray. 1990. *College Sports Inc.: The Athletic Department vs. The University*. New York: Henry Holt and Company.

Thelin, John R. 1994. *Games Colleges Play: Scandal and Reform in Intercollegiate Athletics*. Baltimore: Johns Hopkins University Press.

Thelin, John R. and Wiseman, Lawrence L. 1989. *The Old College Try: Balancing Athletics and Academics in Higher Education*. Washington, D.C.: The George Washington University, Report No. 4.

Tinto, Vincent. 1993. *Leaving College: Rethinking the Causes and Cures of Student Attrition*. Chicago: The University of Chicago Press.

Torpor, Bob. *Marketing Higher Education*. March 1995. Vol. IX, No. 3. Torpor & Associates. Mountain View, CA.

U.S. Department of Labor and The Hudson Institute. 1987. *Workforce 2000*. Washington, DC.

Walker, Chet. 1995. *Long Time Coming: A Black Athlete's Coming-of-Age in America*. New York: Grove Press.

Walton, Gary M. 1992. *Beyond Winning: The Timeless Wisdom of Great Philosopher Coaches*. Champaign, IL: Leisure Press.

Westmeyer, Paul. 1985. *A History of American Higher Education*. Springfield, IL: Charles C. Thomas.

Wingspread Group on Higher Education. 1993. *An American Imperative: Higher Expectations for Higher Education*. Racine, WI: The Johnson Foundation.

Wolff, Alexander. "Broken Beyond Repair" *Sports Illustrated*, 12 June 1995.

INDEX

by Linda Webster